FOODPRINTS

THE STORY OF
WHAT WE EAT

PAULA AYER

annick press
toronto + new york + vancouver

For my parents — P.A.

Edited by Pam Roberston
Copyedited by Linda Pruessen
Proofread by Tanya Trafford
Cover and interior design by Natalie Olsen / Kisscut Design

Annick Press Ltd.

We acknowledge the support of the Canada Council for the Arts, the Ontario Arts Council, and the Government of Canada through the Canada Book Fund (CBF) for our publishing activities.

ONTARIO ARTS COUNCIL
CONSEIL DES ARTS DE L'ONTARIO
an Ontario government agency
un organisme du gouvernement de l'Ontario

Cataloging in Publication
Ayer, Paula, author
Foodprints : the story of what we eat / Paula Ayer.

Includes bibliographical references and index. Issued in print and electronic formats.
ISBN 978-1-55451-718-3 (pbk.).—ISBN 978-1-55451-719-0 (bound).—ISBN 978-1-55451-720-6 (html).—ISBN 978-1-55451-721-3 (pdf)

1. Food—Juvenile literature. I. Title.

TX355.A93 2015   j641.3   C2014-905906-X
                                        C2014-905907-8

Distributed in Canada by:
Firefly Books Ltd.
50 Staples Avenue, Unit 1
Richmond Hill, ON L4B 0A7

Published in the U.S.A. by Annick Press (U.S.) Ltd.
Distributed in the U.S.A. by:
Firefly Books (U.S.) Inc.
P.O. Box 1338
Ellicott Station
Buffalo, NY 14205

Printed in China

Visit us at: **www.annickpress.com**
Follow the author on Twitter: **twitter.com/paulaayer**

Also available in e-book format. Please visit www.annickpress.com/ebooks.html for more details.
Or scan

CONTENTS

WHAT DO YOU THINK OF when you think about food? Your dad's famous burgers, your mom's curry simmering on the stove, or your grandma's cookies baking in the oven? Maybe the pizza slice you're planning to grab after school, or the granola bar you shoved in your mouth between classes? With so many delicious choices when it comes to your next snack or meal, no wonder many of us wrestle with that all-important question: *What should I eat?*

It's easy to take food at face value. It's delicious, you're hungry, you eat it—The End. But if you look a little closer, everything on your plate tells a story. Every morsel of food came from somewhere, and went through a journey—often a fascinating one!—to get to you.

Sometimes those stories stretch back hundreds or thousands of years, to the first people who thought to bury a seed in the ground. The story of any food has many different authors: the farmers who grew the food, the scientists who tinkered with it, the workers who processed it, the companies that sold it, and the person—maybe you, or someone in your family—who cooked it. There are different chapters, sometimes spanning cultures and continents, and twists in the plot, either from decisions or accidents of fate. The food in your own kitchen tells stories about where your family comes from and where you live. If you read between the lines, it might tell you about how much money your family has to spend on food, your culture and traditions, and the things you value. And, of course, it tells you what your taste buds prefer, whether it's sushi or peanut butter sandwiches.

These days, we have more choice about what we eat than ever before. In fact, when it comes to food, you're likely more experienced than your parents. Back when they were kids, meat, potatoes, and veggies was a pretty

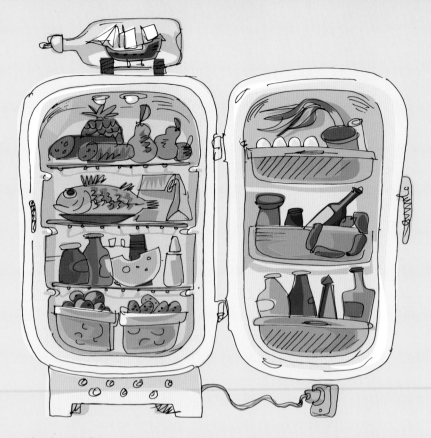

standard meal for many North Americans. Today, you'd be as likely to find pasta, tacos, or a stir-fry on the table. Things have changed outside of the home, too: in an average restaurant you can order meals from cultures around the world, and your local grocery store probably caters to all sorts of food preferences, from organic to gluten-free.

When you were younger, you didn't have to make so many choices about food. You ate what your parents gave you or, if you were lucky, whatever you could convince them to buy. But now that you're older, you're likely making some of your own decisions about what you eat, whether it's by adding to the family grocery list, buying snacks, deciding where to go for lunch with friends, or helping to prepare dinner. And as you get more involved, questions might come up, like: Where does my food come from? How was it made? Is what I'm eating going to make me feel good and keep me healthy? And, what convinced me to eat *this*, instead of something else?

You can learn how to read the stories that food tells. You probably see all sorts of information about food, like ads for soft drinks, nutrition information in school, and Internet lists proclaiming the "best and worst" foods to eat. But the messages often contradict each other, and it can be hard to know which ones to trust. So, while this book won't help you answer the question of what to eat, it *will* give you the tools to understand how to read your food: where it comes from, why it matters, and what you can do to make informed decisions about what ends up on your plate. Throughout the following chapters, we'll look at:

 how our modern, ultra-convenient food system evolved, and whether it lives up to its promises to make our lives better;

the role of the big farms and factories where a lot of our food is produced;

what it takes to be healthy, and how to figure out what nutrition advice you can trust;

the weird science of food, and how people in lab coats are as important as farmers to the modern food system;

how food is sold, and why advertisers crave teens' attention; and

how some people are trying to shape the future of food in positive ways, and what you can do to join in.

There's a huge world of food around you—a world that can be both exciting and confusing. But becoming a good "reader" of food is the first step toward making conscious choices. And you make those choices, whether you realize it or not, every time you sit down to eat.

First, we'll start at the beginning ...

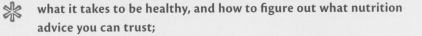

CHAPTER 1

FROM GRAZING TO GLOBAL

LET'S TAKE A TRIP BACK IN TIME—20,000 years back. There are no fast-food restaurants for you to eat in, no coffee shops on every corner, and no grocery stores. In fact, people haven't even figured out how to plant things in the ground to make them grow. Even so, food is one of the central preoccupations of your life, and trying to find it takes most of your waking hours. You spend your days tracking and hunting animals, fishing, or searching for roots, leaves, fruits, seeds, and insects. Next comes cleaning, gutting, skinning, shelling, and pounding—transforming hairy, bony animal carcasses and hard or indigestible plants into things you can actually eat. Food is a constant effort, and you're never sure where it will come from next. The threat of starvation is always near.

Now imagine you're in a modern supermarket. Everywhere you turn there are piles of ripe fruits and vegetables, neatly wrapped cuts of meat, and colorful packages. There are foods that don't grow anywhere near where you live, and foods that were harvested many months earlier. Everything is cleaned, prepared, refined, packaged, and ready to eat. All you need to do is to swish your groceries past the scanner and pull out your wallet.

To someone from the distant past, the way we get our food today would seem miraculous. It would even surprise a time traveler from merely a hundred years ago, when people still grew or raised much of what they ate, and prepackaged food was a luxury. Given the easy access we have today, it's hard not to think we've made amazing progress.

So how exactly did we get here?

THE CAVEMAN DIET

HUMANS ARE OMNIVORES NOW, meaning we can eat both plants and animals. But our ancestors—the pre-humans we descended from in Africa—were mainly vegetarian. Anthropologists can tell from their teeth that they ate fruits, nuts, leaves, bugs, and the occasional small bird, lizard, or mouse. They needed to gather fresh food almost constantly, since they had no way to preserve or store it.

Around 2 million years ago, our ancestors *Homo habilis* were eating some meat in addition to plants, consuming dead birds or mammals they happened to come across. Sometime around half a million years ago, *Homo erectus*—another ancestor—was hunting and killing animals like deer or rhinoceros. By the time we evolved into *Homo sapiens*, around 100,000 years ago, the pursuit of food took some of our ancestors out of Africa and around the globe, to Asia, Europe, Australia, and the Americas. By then, we had figured out how to start fires. Not only did this expand our menu—we could now eat cooked plant leaves, stems, or roots that were indigestible raw—but smoking meat with fire was probably the earliest way humans preserved food so it would stay free of bacteria for longer periods of time.

For several hundred thousand years humans existed like this— hunting animals, fishing, and foraging for whatever edible plants or fruits they could find. Then, around 12,000 years ago, things started to change in a big way.

What was on the Stone Age diet? A little bit of everything! Some of the stranger things our long-ago ancestors consumed: animal guts, tough grasses, papyrus (a reedy plant used to make paper), rhinoceroses, giant rats, and lizards the size of Komodo dragons.

NOW WE'RE COOKING

Some scientists who study early humans believe that the invention of cooked food was a crucial step in our evolution. How? Well, if you're eating only raw food, you have to eat *a whole lot* of it for your body to function properly. Munching on raw celery, for example, actually uses slightly more energy chewing and digesting than it provides to your body as calories (which is why celery is sometimes called a "negative-calorie food"). One scientist has estimated that early humans who consumed only unprocessed, raw food would have had to spend over nine hours a day eating in order to fuel their brains' needs!

But cooking food acts as a sort of "pre-digestion," making it softer and easier for our bodies to absorb. So the theory is that once cooked foods became a larger part of our diet, the energy we previously spent gnawing on raw leaves and roots was redirected to making our brains bigger and smarter.

GETTING AGRICULTURED

THAT CHANGE, which was most likely triggered by the end of the last Ice Age around 11,700 years ago, was the birth of agriculture. For the first time, people began to grow edible plants rather than relying on what they found in the wild. The early center of agricultural activity was the Fertile Crescent, a semicircle of land bordering the Mediterranean Sea and the Persian Gulf. It's an area that boasts mountains, marshlands, rivers, and even desert, and it had a more moderate climate back then, allowing many types of plants to flourish.

The emergence of agriculture wasn't really a sudden change. Earlier peoples had been managing the foods they ate for some time, with techniques like adding nutrients to the soil through the use of fire, and tending fruit and nut trees. Over hundreds and thousands of years, these methods gradually became more intensive and organized.

People who had hunted wild animals, like sheep, goats, and cattle, began to raise those animals instead. People who had gathered legumes and wild grains, like barley, rice, and wheat, eventually started planting seeds. And the more they learned about the process—what types of animals were easiest to raise, for example, and what types of grains, fruits, or vegetables were sweetest, biggest, or easiest to pick—the better at it they got.

It's natural that agriculture developed in places where food resources were plentiful enough that people could stay put for a while. That way, they could cultivate plants and animals as a backup plan for the times when there wasn't much to hunt or forage. Over the next few thousand years, agriculture spread to Europe, Asia, and parts of Africa, and separately developed in the Americas. The tribes of southwestern and eastern North America, for instance, domesticated crops like squash and corn as early as 11,000 years ago. But in many places, people still relied on hunting and foraging for food. As late as 1500 CE, there were still a large number of hunter-gatherer groups in the Americas, Australia, and parts of Africa and Asia.

In the centuries that followed, other advances in farming and food came along. Hoes and digging sticks were used to break the ground. Farmers used livestock to tread seeds into the dirt. People learned how to rotate crops to improve soil quality, used natural fertilizers like manure, and developed forms of irrigation for watering, all of which helped increase the amount of food they could produce. They also came up with better ways to store grain, like silo pits in the ground and storehouses called granaries, to keep it away from animals and to prevent it from getting moldy.

THE ACCIDENTAL GRAIN

Can you imagine life with no bread, bagels, pasta, or cookies? Our ancient ancestors certainly could! When they wanted something delicious and comforting, they likely turned to a bowl of fern soup or a nice leg of wild boar. Then wheat was domesticated, one of the first crops to be cultivated by humans, and the rest is history.

Wheat may be a central ingredient in modern life, but that's more a result of chance than planning. Here's why: when wild wheat is ripe, its grains fall to the ground, allowing the following year's growth to seed itself. Domesticated wheat, however, stays on its stem. That makes it easier to harvest—but means it can't reproduce without human intervention. Scientists think the difference is the result of a random genetic mutation in wild wheat that happened right around the time people were starting to cultivate wheat. If early farmers hadn't been replanting the easier-to-pick mutant seeds, that strain would have died out. Instead, it became the basis for the wheat we eat today.

Have you got the guts for agriculture? Through evolution, some groups of humans actually developed genetic differences that helped them digest starchy foods, like wheat and rice, or milk from cows and goats. So if you can eat a cheese sandwich without getting a stomachache, thank the ancient grain and dairy farmers in your family tree!

URBAN FARE

THANKS TO THESE NEW WAYS OF GETTING FOOD, people no longer had to move from place to place in pursuit of their next meal. They needed to stay in one spot in order to farm, so the first permanent communities, and then cities, grew around agricultural hot spots. And just as agriculture made cities necessary, without agriculture, cities couldn't exist.

ROTATION INNOVATION

Early farmers practiced a technique called crop rotation, meaning they grew different crops in the same field at different times of the year. When grains grow, they take nitrogen out of the soil. Legumes like lentils or beans add nitrogen. By switching back and forth between the two, farmers made sure that the soil's nutrients were replenished and the land stayed useful for longer.

Ancient Syrians were using a form of crop rotation around 8000 BCE, though it's unclear if this was by accident or on purpose. Later, farmers in Rome and the Middle East used a "three-field" system: field one would be planted with grains, field two with legumes, and field three would be left to rest, with nothing planted. They'd rotate the crops every year.

The harvest was the most important part of life in ancient cities like Ur, in what's now Iraq. By 4000 BCE, people there were growing a wide range of crops, including barley, wheat, flax, apples, plums, and grapes, as well as raising livestock for meat and milk. Nearly half of the city's population worked in this early food industry, whether as farm laborers, supervisors, or record-keepers. At the center of food activity was the temple, where city administrators would organize the harvest, offer grain to the gods, and distribute the rest to citizens.

Food production had to keep pace with growing cities, as populations in urban centers in Egypt, Iraq, China, India, and Europe soared into the hundreds of thousands. By the first century CE, Rome was the biggest city in the history of the world, with 1 million people, and its population's appetite had gotten too big to handle. Produce, like artichokes, onions, figs, and grapes, could be carted in from the surrounding countryside.

The gods are hungry! Many cultures throughout history have sacrificed food to religious deities as a way to appease or pay tribute to them. Animals were often ritually slaughtered, while grain, fruits, and other foods could be burned or left as offerings.

THE FIRST SHOPPING LISTS?

Agriculture was crucial to the development of modern civilization in many ways. Believe it or not, the birth of agriculture is thought to have led to the development of writing, which grew out of the symbols used by scribes to keep track of grain and livestock production.

And live animals and poultry could be walked in from outside the city to markets, where they would be slaughtered and sold. But transporting enough grain for 1 million people over long distances—by cart and horse, over bumpy, unpaved roads—was a serious challenge. Thankfully, Rome had access to the sea, so grain could be imported from North Africa, the Middle East, and the rest of coastal Europe.

In fact, Rome's efforts to build its empire—which eventually encircled the Mediterranean Sea and covered much of Europe—were motivated in part by a need for food. Ancient Romans would set out on what one expert has called a "militarized shopping spree," conquering a city to gain control of its grain resources. For the first time, one city's food needs were shaping the politics, environment, and economies of other cities and countries, sometimes in violent ways.

Even when food was shipped in from a distant land, it was bought and sold in streets and public places, something that wouldn't change until the 20th century. Food was the center of social activity, and the market was a place where citizens would meet and talk daily. It would have been hard to feel disconnected from your food, or where it came from.

TRADE YA!

FOOD HAS ALWAYS PROVIDED A LINK between different cultures. Today, that's obvious every time you're in the food court trying to decide whether you want Thai food or burritos. But the exchange of ingredients and dishes from one culture to another has been going on for hundreds of years. Food has not just become global; it was one of the biggest reasons *for* global trade. The pursuit of spices—black pepper, cinnamon, and cloves in particular—was a major reason for European exploration of Asia, and led to the accidental "discovery" of America while searching for a sea route to the East.

When European explorers and settlers showed up in the so-called New World, they brought along all sorts of foods that didn't exist there yet, like apples, oranges, bananas, coffee, wheat, and rice. They also took home indigenous American plants that were unknown in Europe, such as corn, potatoes, and tomatoes. This swapping of treats is sometimes called the Columbian Exchange, after explorer Christopher Columbus, and it represents the first real globalization of food. Imagine—before that, there were no oranges in Florida or pineapples in Hawaii, and no potatoes in Ireland or tomatoes in Italy!

Europeans also brought domesticated "food" animals like cows, pigs, and chickens to the Americas, as well as horses—which would revolutionize work and transportation. Before then, Native tribes hadn't ever raised animals for food; they'd always hunted wild animals like deer, rabbits, and bison.

RISE OF THE MACHINES

I T WASN'T UNTIL THE INDUSTRIAL REVOLUTION in the late 18th century that the next big changes in food production happened. Inventions like the seed drill (which distributed seeds at even intervals), steam-powered plows and tractors (for loosening the soil), and mechanical combine harvesters and threshers (for collecting and separating grain) allowed farmers to use less human labor, and led to speeds and scales of production that were impossible before.

Ice delivery! Before fridges, many people used insulated containers called iceboxes to keep fresh food like milk and butter from spoiling. Every day the iceman would go door to door with fresh blocks of ice to refill them. Other places to keep food cold: cellars, caves, and boxes buried under rivers or streams.

The way food got from farms to cities also changed dramatically. In the 1800s, railroads started to crisscross Europe, the U.S., and Canada. Grain and animals could now be transported by land from much farther away. And when refrigerated rail cars showed up in the late 1800s, perishable foods like produce, meat, and dairy could be shipped long distances, too. In the U.S., the ability to ship fruits and vegetables across the country changed the agricultural map. Different regions started to specialize in different types of produce: grapes in California, peaches in Georgia, tomatoes in Mississippi, melons in the Southwest.

CHEMICAL HELPERS

It wasn't only machines that sped up the production of food. Synthetic fertilizers (made from chemicals, as opposed to "organic" fertilizers like animal manure, bone meal, or food compost) were developed in the early 1900s, and helped crops grow faster and bigger. The discovery of vitamins in the 1920s meant animals could be raised indoors (where they were protected from weather and predators) and given synthetic supplements like vitamin D, which mammals produce naturally when exposed to sunlight. With the development of antibiotics and vaccines, farmers could keep greater numbers of animals close together with less risk of diseases caused by crowding.

INFOBITES
FOOD THEN AND NOW

PORTION OF LABOR FORCE IN U.S. THAT WORKS ON FARMS

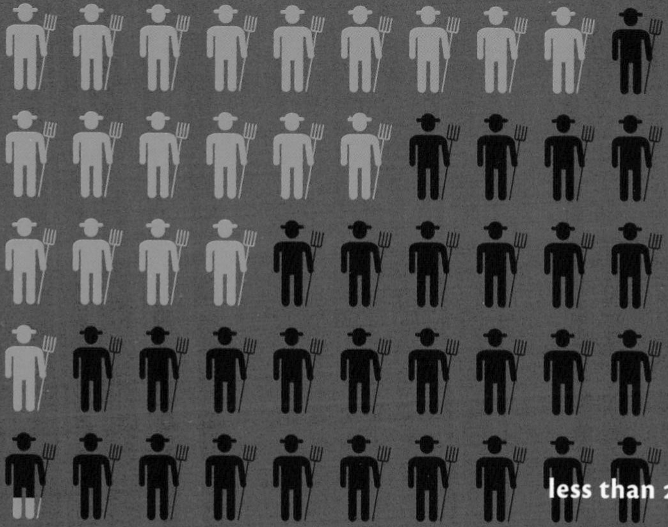

1790 — 9 in 10

1850 — 6 in 10

1900 — 4 in 10

1950 — 1 in 10

Today — less than 2 in 100

AMOUNT OF FOOD PRODUCED BY EACH FARM WORKER

1940

enough for **11** people

Today

enough for **90** people

NUMBER OF FARMS IN THE U.S.

1920

6.5 million
average area 60 hectares
(148 acres)

Today

2.5 million
average area 176 hectares
(435 acres)

Identical cans are filled with peas in a Wisconsin factory in the 1930s.

The invention of rail also meant that cities could grow larger and larger. Before, a city's size was restricted by how much food could be grown in and right around it. If the city only had the land and resources to produce enough food for, say, 100,000 people, the population needed to stay at that size for everyone to be fed. Places with access to the sea, like Rome hundreds of years earlier, could ship in food from farther away, but conquering and pillaging cities for their grain had gone out of style. Once rail made it easier to bring in food from across the continent, everything changed. And as more and more people poured into cities, the growth and production of food moved further out.

By the beginning of the 20th century, factories were also part of the food scene. Everything from canned fruits and vegetables, preserves, packaged cereals (like Kellogg's Corn Flakes, which hit the market in 1906), crackers, and chocolate bars were identically manufactured and packaged on assembly lines, then distributed nationwide. Food was becoming not simply something grown on a farm and prepared in kitchens, but a product, mass-produced and sold by large companies, many of which would eventually grow into huge international corporations.

A crop duster spraying a field of wheat. New fertilizers, pesticides, and grain varieties developed during the Green Revolution helped bump up food production.

THE GREEN REVOLUTION

AFTER **WORLD WAR II,** agriculture really went into high gear. From the 1940s to the '60s, there were all sorts of new inventions that helped farmers grow more food, faster: new types of grains, stronger fertilizers and pesticides, and better techniques for irrigating and managing crops. Innovations like these were such a success that global food production in 1975 was *16 times* higher than it had been in 1820, even though there were only about 4 times more people on Earth!

Those changes helped save lot of people—over a billion worldwide! — from famine. Food shortages in India, for example, were threatening mass starvation at the beginning of the 1960s. So the Indian goverment worked with food scientists to grow a new variety of rice that yielded 10 times more grain than regular rice. India's rice production tripled over the next 30 years, and prices fell.

INFOBITES
HUNGER

Today, approximately 1 in 8 people in the world—around 842 million—don't have enough to eat. But that number has actually gone down over the years.

PERCENTAGE OF PEOPLE WORLDWIDE CONSIDERED CHRONICALLY UNDERNOURISHED:

37%	28%	20%	16%	17%	16%	12%
1970	1980	1990	2005	2007	2009	2012

THE FUTURE

By 2050, it's estimated that:

There will be twice as many people living in cities as there are today.

We'll be consuming twice as much meat as we do today.

Shorter is better? For crops, maybe! Traditional types of rice and wheat grow tall, which blocks the sun from neighboring plants unless they're spaced widely apart. One Green Revolution advance was to develop shorter plants that could be packed together more closely, which meant more grain could be grown.

The starvation crisis was averted, and India is now one of the world's biggest exporters of rice. There were similar success stories with rice in the Philippines, and wheat in Mexico.

Most of the food available in our supermarkets today comes from methods of industrial farming developed during this period of phenomenal growth, known as the Green Revolution. But the techniques needed to produce food on such a large scale have also been criticized for having long-term effects on the environment, human health, and food sustainability, as we'll see in the next chapter. Driven by the constant need to lower expenses and produce more, industrial agriculture has created some strange paths between our food and us. For instance, rather than growing a crop locally, it can be cheaper to grow a giant field of soybeans or rice in Brazil or China, ship the food halfway around the world to be processed into something else, and then ship it to yet another spot to be sold. Maybe more than anything else, the Green Revolution has shaped the way the world eats today, for better and worse.

THE BIRTH
OF SELF-SERVE

HOW OFTEN DOES YOUR MOM
or dad visit the grocery store each
week, or zip in on the way home
from work or a family outing to pick up a few
items? Have you ever been asked to ride your
bike to the corner store for a loaf of bread or
some milk? Most of us can't imagine not being
able to make a quick stop when we want a snack
or need some last-minute dinner ingredient,
but the modern grocery store is actually a fairly recent invention.

When Europeans first settled North America, the center of food
activity was the trading post, a store usually built along a traditional
trade route. It sold everything the new settler needed: clothing,
furniture, tools, and household items, as well as basic foods. Later,
these trading posts evolved into general stores, where people would
buy their dry goods, like flour, canned foods, dried beans, and spices.
For fresh foods, you'd go to the source: meat from a butcher, who
killed and prepared animals himself, milk from a local dairy, and fruits
and vegetables from a greengrocer or farm stand. Many families also
grew their own vegetables and raised chickens for eggs. You'd have
to go to three or four different places to get what you needed for a
meal, but back then, most women didn't work outside of the home,
and the tasks of getting, preparing, and cooking food took up a good
part of their day.

In old-fashioned general stores, which were common in North
America through the 1800s and early 1900s, all the goods would
be stacked behind a counter. Rather than browsing the shelves and

Customers could pick their own groceries from the shelves at Piggly Wiggly stores like this one, in Tennessee, around 1919.

choosing items yourself, you'd give your shopping list to a clerk, who would fill your order. And goods didn't come in neat packages, the way they do now—they were mostly in bulk containers, so the clerk would have to measure out the amount of flour or sugar you wanted, weigh it, calculate the price, and wrap it up. It was all a little time-consuming, but at least you'd get to know your grocery store clerk pretty well!

It wasn't until 1919 that the first "self-service" grocery store, called Piggly Wiggly, was opened, in Memphis, Tennessee. The novelty of the shopping experience, in which customers picked their own prepackaged, prepriced products off the shelves, allowed the store to get by with fewer clerks, and customers to have more choice. (These stores were sometimes called "groceterias": as in a cafeteria, you selected your own food.) The ideas of brands, packaging, and advertising became very important (more on this in chapter 5), and the self-service model quickly spread.

Clarence Saunders, who started the Piggly Wiggly chain, also invented the first fully automated grocery store, called Keedoozle, in 1937. Customers would select groceries by sticking a key into labeled holes on giant cabinets, and their items would be dispensed automatically through a complicated system of electric circuits, ticker tape, and conveyor belts. Unfortunately, the technology often malfunctioned, and the Keedoozle concept was dead within a few years. But Saunders's idea lives on in modern vending machines and self-checkouts at grocery stores.

FROM SUPER...

N THE 1920S, grocery stores started to look a little more like the places we would recognize today. Some started to sell perishable items like fruit, vegetables, meat, and dairy, as well as dry goods, though the stores were still relatively small. The 1930s saw the birth of the first supermarkets: large, self-service grocery stores with separate departments for meat, dairy, baked goods, and more. These were not independent stores, but chains: one company would own dozens, hundreds, or even thousands of stores that operated under one name, either nationally or in a particular region. Thanks to their size and the scale of their operations—one supermarket could sell as much as 100 regular grocery stores—these chains could offer a greater selection of products for a cheaper price than their smaller counterparts.

This was also the age of the automobile, which meant that more and more people could drive to grocery stores instead of walking, and carry

home greater amounts of food. Because supermarkets were so much larger than traditional grocery stores—and now needed more space for parking—they had to be built near the outskirts of cities, rather than downtown or in residential neighborhoods. Though many people still shopped at smaller grocery stores or general stores, supermarkets became more popular through the Great Depression, when a weak economy left most Americans with less money to spend on food. In 1935, there were only 300 supermarkets in the entire U.S.—by the end of the decade, there were nearly 5,000!

After World War II, as middle-class families fled cities for newly built suburbs, supermarkets really took off. The 1950s and '60s were the golden age of the supermarket, with colorful new stores opening regularly, serving a prosperous clientele and selling all manner of bright and appealing packaged foods. By the 1970s, many traditional corner grocery stores were going out of business.

INFOBITES
FOOD SPENDING

PERCENTAGE OF TOTAL HOUSEHOLD SPENDING GOING TO FOOD EATEN AT HOME, BY COUNTRY (2014):

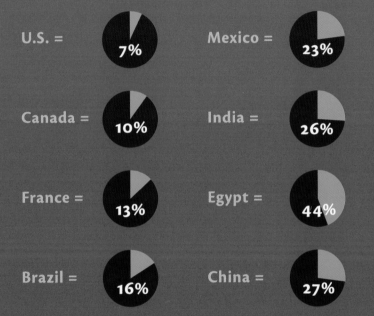

U.S. = 7%

Mexico = 23%

Canada = 10%

India = 26%

France = 13%

Egypt = 44%

Brazil = 16%

China = 27%

PERCENTAGE OF HOUSEHOLD INCOME SPENT ON FOOD (AT HOME AND OUT) IN THE U.S., BY YEAR:

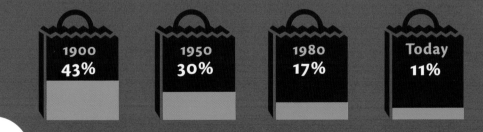

1900 43%

1950 30%

1980 17%

Today 11%

...TO HYPER

THEN, IN THE 1980S AND '90S, things went supersized. Regional supermarket chains merged to create national or global companies. And big-box stores like Walmart and Target got into the food business, creating so-called hypermarkets. A kind of turbo-charged version of the old-fashioned general store, a hypermarket boasts everything you could possibly need under one roof, from milk and bread to jeans and furniture.

Hypermarkets often carry a mind-boggling 200,000—or more! — different brands and merchandise items. Food goes through the company's giant distribution center (which cuts costs, since the company doesn't have to pay an outside distributor) before being shipped to individual stores in the company's own trucks. The name of the game for these stores is "high volume, low margin": they undercut competitors by selling a lot of each product at a lower price.

Let's crunch the numbers to see how this works: Say you own a small store that sells apples, among other things. You might buy apples from a farmer for $1 a pound. To keep your store running while paying your overhead expenses—like rent, staffing, and heat—you need to sell the apples for $1.75 a pound. A hypermarket, on the other hand, might charge the customer only $1.10 for those same apples. They're not making as much off each sale (it's a lower profit margin), but they make up for it by selling thousands of pounds of apples a day!

One out of every four dollars spent on groceries in the U.S. is spent at Walmart! The hypermarket chain is the biggest grocery retailer in the world, with over $244 billion worth of food sold in 2012.

E-FOOD

SO WHERE WILL WE GO FROM SUPER- AND HYPERMARKETS?
Well, it's possible the grocery store of the future won't even
have walls. These days, you can skip the store and buy all sorts
of food online. Depending on where you live, you might be able to
order a weekly box of fresh fruits and veggies from a local supplier,
a specialty ingredient you need for a recipe, or a favorite regional
or international food you can't find in your area. And even some
traditional grocery stores are going electronic, allowing customers to
order online and replacing checkout staff with self-scanning machines.

E-groceries have advantages: less money spent on staff and store
space means (in theory at least) lower prices for shoppers, and more
selection. Supermarkets don't have to worry about being put out of
business yet, though: as of 2013, only about 1 percent of Americans'
spending on food was done online.
But that might change as Internet
shopping becomes more and
more mainstream and delivery
times improve.

FOOD FOR THOUGHT

When you're sitting down to dinner tonight, take a minute to look at your plate (or bowl, or takeout container) and think about a few questions. There are no right or wrong answers—this is just an exercise to get your mind thinking about where your food comes from, and maybe start a family discussion:

Which foods, if any, are likely to have come from your state or province? Which ones were probably grown or produced farther away? Take a look at produce stickers or food packaging to check.

Who bought the food and who prepared it? Your mom or dad? Your grandparents or you? Or a restaurant employee?

What steps did the food have to go through before reaching you—cleaning, packaging, transporting, cooking?

Where did your meal come from? A supermarket, or restaurant, or farmers' market? Was anything on your plate grown or made by someone you know?

What has been made from scratch (e.g., from ingredients like a tomato or butter and flour) and what came already prepared or partially prepared (e.g., a can of soup or a box of macaroni and cheese)?

CHAPTER 2

FOOD INC.

YOU'VE GOT THE MUNCHIES, so you walk into a store and scan the shelves full of snacks, fruit, and bottled drinks. You select a granola bar or bag of chips, glancing at the little logo on the package as you walk to the counter. Chances are you can trace your snack back to 1 of about 10 huge companies— international businesses like Nestlé, Kraft, PepsiCo, and General Mills, each of which own dozens of smaller brands. In fact, you could link almost every food or drink in the store to one of a handful of multinational companies that control a big slice of all the food produced, sold, and eaten worldwide.

Food is big business, and as with any business, the most important goal is making a profit. That means there's constant pressure on food companies, and those who supply them, to produce as much food as possible as cheaply as possible. But the cheapest ways of producing food aren't always the healthiest or the best—for the environment, for the animals raised for meat, milk, and eggs, for food workers, or for you. Let's take a look at the modern farm system and see why.

CONSOLIDATE, INTEGRATE

HOW DID FOOD GET SO BIG? To understand, it helps to know a little about the business world, and two trends over the last few decades that have changed the way things are done. The first, consolidation, is what happens when companies join together to form larger alliances. PepsiCo, the American company best known for its Pepsi soft drink, owns dozens of smaller companies, including Quaker, Frito Lay, Tropicana, and Gatorade. So if you had cereal and juice for breakfast, tortilla chips at lunch, and a soda after school, your food dollars might all end up in the pocket of the same CEO. That's consolidation in action!

The second trend is vertical integration—where a corporation buys up other companies that are important to its business so it can exert more control and lower costs. In the food industry, this means one company can control everything from the seeds planted to the fertilizers used on them to the processing, transportation, and even selling of the final product.

How does this work? Let's say a big multinational company has an agreement with a farmer to raise animals for food. The same company could sell the farmer its own feed and medicines, and require him to follow certain methods of raising the animals. And when the animals are ready for slaughter, the company will pick them up, transport them to a slaughterhouse they own, process the meat, and distribute it using their own shipping system.

Harvesting a soybean field in Brazil

This arrangement certainly has its benefits. It means that food costs are kept down, which helps consumers. It can also mean that the large company, which has the resources to research the most efficient ways to produce or grow food, shares its knowledge with farmers. On the other hand, this system takes power away from the people who actually produce the food, and often gives it to corporate executives who might have no direct experience farming or raising animals. Farmers have less control over what they produce, how they produce it, and what they charge for it. And that's not all. Since the large company's goal is to produce greater amounts of food at lower prices, vertical integration leads to fewer small- and medium-sized farms, and more megafarms and feedlots. It also leads to less variety in the crops that are grown and the breeds of animals that are raised. It's cheaper and easier to grow six fields of the same kind of potatoes, for example, than to grow six entirely different crops. With nothing but one type of potatoes on his mind, the farmer can plant, fertilize, and harvest everything the same way.

THE SPICE OF LIFE

HAVE YOU EVER HEARD THE EXPRESSION "variety is the spice of life"? It reminds us that the more things and experiences we're exposed to, the better our lives can be. As it turns out, people aren't the only ones who like to spice things up. In nature, variety is usually considered a very good thing indeed. "Biodiversity" basically means variety of life—in other words, how many different kinds of species or breeds exist in an environment. A very biodiverse environment features more plant growth, fewer pests, and more stable animal populations than environments that are not as biodiverse.

Biodiversity used to be a natural part of our food system. You might think one pork chop is pretty much the same as any other pork chop, and a carrot is just a carrot. But traditionally, small, independent farmers and ranchers raised hundreds of different breeds of cattle, pigs, and chickens, and grew all sorts of fruit and vegetable varieties, like purple beans, white carrots, or striped tomatoes. Many of these had evolved to suit their particular surroundings (for example, withstanding hot climates, humidity, or parasites) and had unique flavors and qualities.

POTATO PERILS

One of the worst food disasters of all time, the Irish potato famine, shows the dangers of relying on a single type of crop. By the 1800s, the potato, brought from South America over to Europe by Spaniards, was the staple food in Ireland. At the time, the Irish lived under British control, and poor Irish laborers had to rent out small plots of land from English landowners to grow their food. Potatoes were a cheap source of calories that could be grown in a small area. Most of the potatoes planted were Lumpers, a variety known for producing big crops. But when a deadly fungus that the Lumper was susceptible to spread through the food supply in 1845, it wiped out the entire potato crop. Within seven years a million Irish people died of starvation, and another million were forced to leave the country.

Similar threats to our food supply still exist today. Stem rust is a fungus that has been slowly spreading across the globe since 1999. It has the potential to destroy almost 90 percent of the world's wheat, which would leave a billion people in danger of starvation. Scientists are working to develop new strains of wheat resistant to stem rust.

DESIGNER GENES

TODAY, MUCH OF THAT DIVERSITY HAS BEEN LOST. Modern genetics companies like Cargill and ConAgra own the rights to certain breeds or strains of animals and plants, and hold contracts with big livestock producers to sell them young animals or genetic material. That means the market has become much more controlled. In the U.S., for instance, only two companies control 90 percent of the genes for egg-laying chickens.

It also means fewer breeds are being raised. Practically all beef now comes from only 10 breeds of cattle (it used to come from dozens) and almost all white eggs in the U.S. come from one type of chicken. All but two breeds of pig in the U.S. are considered threatened or close to extinction. Why are certain breeds preferred by the food industry? It's generally not because their meat is tastier or healthier, but for the speed at which they can gain enough weight to be slaughtered.

Birds and bees might do it, but modern cows and pigs usually don't! In the U.S. today, 80 percent of pigs, 95 percent of dairy cows, and 100 percent of commercially raised turkeys are born from artificial insemination.

Animals are amazingly adaptable. The zebu, a type of cattle native to South Asia, is well suited to hot climates because of its ability to produce more cooling sweat than other cattle. And the North Ronaldsay sheep in the Orkney Islands, off the north coast of Scotland, have learned to survive for several months a year on an all-seaweed diet—the only food available to them.

Plants are being affected too. Some food experts say that nearly 100,000 plant species are in danger of extinction, and thousands of different genetic varieties of fruits, vegetables, grains, and beans have disappeared. In the 1800s, for example, 7,000 varieties of apples grew in the U.S.; today there are fewer than 100. It's estimated that 90 percent of the fruit and vegetable varieties that used to exist in the U.S. have been lost.

So what's the problem if a breed of pig or variety of tomato disappears? For one thing, the best-tasting or most nutritious varieties are usually pushed aside in favor of ones that store and ship well. Even more important, scientists concerned about food security—making sure people have access to enough food over the long term—argue that a less diverse food system is more vulnerable to risk. Things like disease, pests, fungus, or climate change can have devastating effects on our food supply if they wipe out a key variety of plant or animal. And they're more likely to destroy organisms that are genetically similar. Growing a wider variety of crops and animals spreads out the risk.

STORING DIVERSITY

Many people are working to restore diversity to the food landscape:

❋ Small farmers in North America and abroad have brought back "heirloom" varieties of tomatoes, apples, beans, and other foods—old varieties that are no longer used in conventional modern agriculture. These have become popular items at farmers' markets and independent grocery stores.

❋ Some companies have made a name for themselves by promoting rare varieties as gourmet foods. A company called Rancho Gordo, based in California, works with farmers in Mexico to grow traditional indigenous crops like heirloom beans and seeds that were close to extinction.

❋ There are approximately 1,400 seed banks around the world where wild and out-of-use seed varieties are gathered and stored. The largest, in London, England, stores nearly 2 billion seeds (from over 33,000 species) in a huge, multilevel underground vault. Geneticists and food scientists working for the bank have successfully re-introduced hundreds of endangered plant species into the wild.

INFOBITES
BIG FOOD

IN THE U.S., THE TOP FOUR LIVESTOCK COMPANIES IN EACH INDUSTRY CONTROL:

8 in 10 cows

6 in 10 pigs

5 in 10 chickens

SUBSIDIES

YEARLY SUBSIDIES PAID BY THE U.S. GOVERNMENT:

Meat and dairy farmers:

Fruit and vegetable growers:

$38 BILLION

$17 MILLION

CLIMATE EFFECTS

YOU'VE PROBABLY HEARD A LOT ABOUT CLIMATE CHANGE— long-term changes in global weather patterns that are caused by increasing levels of greenhouse gases, which trap heat in the earth's atmosphere. One of the reasons climate change causes so much worry is because of how it might affect our food supply. Climate change means more extreme weather, like droughts, heat waves, and flooding— all of which can be catastrophic for crops.

The effects on food are already a reality in North America. In 2014, California had its driest year since the Middle Ages, and climate scientists say extreme droughts in the state will become more common. That's bad news for farmers, who use about 80 percent of the state's water. It's also bad news for everyone else, because California grows about half of all fruits and vegetables eaten in the U.S.— including over 90 percent of strawberries, grapes, broccoli, and tomatoes—and produces one-fifth of the country's dairy. Drought conditions have led to lower yields and higher food prices across North America.

Around the world, scientists warn that millions of people could face starvation because of climate-related food shortages unless governments take action to cut greenhouse gas emissions. In the food industry, people have taken notice: in 2014, the heads of 8 of the 10 biggest international food and beverage companies urged world leaders to do something about climate change.

PESTS BE GONE

WHEN YOU GROW A BIG FIELD with one type of crop, it also tends to attract a lot of pests. Pesticides are chemicals that kill or deter pests that prey on crops, and large monoculture farms tend to need more of them than smaller farms that use traditional methods like crop rotation. Worldwide, we use an estimated 2 billion kilograms (5 billion pounds) of pesticides in agriculture every year—that's more than the combined weight of the entire human population of Texas! About a fifth of that amount is used in the U.S.

Chemical pesticides are one reason for the huge increase in global food production over the last hundred years: more pests killed means less food is damaged or lost. Many farmers and scientists say avoiding pesticides would result in poorer production, rising food prices, and shortages, which in turn would lead to increased world hunger.

But pesticide use also has its risks:

* The World Health Organization estimates that pesticides poison 3 million agriculture workers each year, including around 20,000 in the U.S.

* Pesticides residues seep into the soil and groundwater, and sprayed pesticides can drift through the air. This can threaten wildlife in the surrounding area.

* Certain kinds of pesticides kill honeybees. Honeybees help grow about a third of the world's food supply, transferring pollen between flowers so they can produce food. The bee population has already dropped sharply and if it keeps going, many types of food crops, including apples, berries, almonds, and melons, could die off.

* When animals at the bottom of the food chain (like bugs or rodents) eat or come into contact with pesticides, they unknowingly set off a chain reaction. All of the poison they've absorbed is passed on when they are eaten by animals higher up the chain (like small birds or fish). Now the poison builds up in the system of those mid-food-chain animals. And guess what happens when they become food for animals above them in the chain (like birds of prey or mammals)? You're right if you said the poisons become even more concentrated (this is called "bioaccumulation").

* Pests can become resistant to pesticides, which means stronger chemicals or larger amounts are needed to kill them.

* Pesticide residues on food can cause reactions in people who eat the food. Many people are concerned about the long-term health effects of consuming even tiny amounts of these chemicals.

Save the bees! The organization Avaaz has collected nearly 3 million signatures for an online petition urging world leaders to ban pesticides called neonicotinoids, which have been shown to harm honeybees. In 2014, the European Union was the first to announce a ban on these poisons.

Pesticides can travel a long way! Every year, over a million metric tons of chemical pesticide and fertilizer residue from farms in the U.S. Midwest flow down the Mississippi River into the Gulf of Mexico. That causes a "dead zone" of algae to bloom each spring, creating an environment in which no marine life can survive. In some years the Gulf of Mexico dead zone has been bigger than the state of Connecticut!

PESTICIDES PAST

Pesticides are hardly new; people have been using different substances to protect crops for at least 4,000 years. Some of these less-than-wholesome bug-killers included arsenic (a popular murder weapon from detective novels) and lead (a toxic metal that causes side effects ranging from abdominal pain and muscle weakness to death).

In the 1950s, DDT became the most widely used pesticide in the U.S. In the 1960s, biologist and writer Rachel Carson wrote a highly influential book called *Silent Spring*, which revealed that spraying DDT to kill insects on crops was seriously threatening birds and other animals. Chemical companies launched a vicious campaign to discredit Carson, portraying her as a crazy tree-hugger. But governments eventually listened, and DDT is now banned for use in agriculture, though it's still used to kill mosquitoes for malaria prevention in some countries.

DDT was even sprayed directly onto the uniforms of U.S. soldiers to protect them from disease-carrying pests such as lice.

ORGANIC GROWTH

SOME PEOPLE WHO ARE CONCERNED about pesticide use prefer to buy food that's certified "organically grown," meaning that no synthetic pesticides or fertilizers have been used to grow it. (Food grown with chemical fertilizers and pesticides is often called "conventionally grown.") Farmers growing organic food use other methods to manage pests, like crop rotation, natural pesticides derived from plants, growing other plants that repel pests, and encouraging the presence of insects (like ladybugs) that keep pests under control.

Organic produce is usually associated with small family farms, but increasing demand has led to the growth of large-scale, nationwide organic companies. Some of these "big organic" companies have been criticized for using many of the same techniques as big conventional operations—such as monocultures to maximize yield, and long-distance transportation. But defenders say the increasing scale of organic agriculture is a good development because it brings down the price of organic produce, and makes it accessible to more people.

KING CORN...

YOU'RE SITTING DOWN TO A BIG BREAKFAST: yogurt, granola, scrambled eggs, toast and margarine, fruit drink, the works. But corn and soybeans? Not likely, right? Wrong! It's entirely likely that those two ingredients are in everything on your plate.

In the North American food system, corn is king. Look in your cupboard or on a supermarket shelf and try to find something that *doesn't* contain corn or an ingredient made from it: corn oil, corn flour, corn starch, corn sweeteners (including high-fructose corn syrup, golden syrup, invert sugar, fructose, and dextrose), along with difficult names like maltodextrin (used as a thickener), and food additives diglycerides and monoglycerides.

Corn turns up in flavored yogurt, salad dressing, margarine, cereals, cookies, crackers, gum, and soft drinks, as well as all sorts of non-food products like toothpaste and cosmetics. It's also fed to the cows and chickens we consume as meat; it's even fed to farmed salmon.

Why is corn everywhere? For one, it's cheap—and it's cheap because the U.S. produces so much of it. In the 1970s, the government introduced bills meant to lower the skyrocketing prices of food. They paid farmers to grow more corn, which kept the price of the crop artificially low. Since then, the corn harvest in the U.S. has increased from 4 billion to 10 billion bushels a year, and today corn farms receive about $4 billion a year from the government, over one-fifth of all the money paid to support U.S. farmers. While defenders of these kinds of subsidies say they support farmers and keep the food system stable, critics say that subsidies encourage people to eat too much of one kind of food, and that the increase of ingredients like high-fructose corn syrup in the American diet is one reason for rising rates of obesity and type 2 diabetes.

...AND QUEEN SOY

IF CORN IS KING, then soy is definitely queen—the second crop that rules our food system. Soybeans are high in protein and have traditionally been a big part of the Asian diet, since they are used to make tofu, soymilk, and miso, among other foods. Today, soybeans are widely grown because they're cheap and produce more protein by area than any other product. Like corn, soy has a huge number of uses; it's a main ingredient in plant-based meat and dairy substitutes and turns up in a variety of processed foods (as soybean oil, soy flour, texturized soy protein, and soy lecithin, and other forms). In the U.S., so much land is used to grow soybeans that if you put it all together, it would cover an area bigger than the state of Arizona! In Brazil, the second-largest producer, environmental groups have criticized huge soybean farms for destroying the Amazon rainforest. So where do all those beans end up? About 85 percent of the world soybean crop is processed into oil—used in cooking, as vehicle fuel, or for industrial uses—and ground into feed for animals.

Corn and soy have advantages as cattle feed: they help fatten up animals faster than grass, require less land than grass-fed cattle, and create a taste and a fattier composition that Americans tend to prefer. Seventy-five years ago it took four to five years for a cow to grow large enough for slaughter. Today, thanks to the heavier diet and synthetic growth hormones, it takes a little over a year.

DIRTY AND CLEAN

The Environmental Working Group publishes a list of the fruits and vegetables most likely to have harmful pesticide residues, and those that generally have lower residues. Whenever possible, try to buy these foods organic:

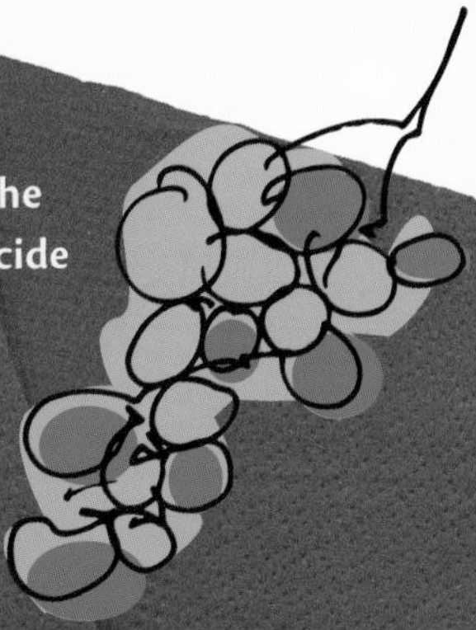

- Apples
- Celery
- Cherry tomatoes
- Cucumbers
- Grapes
- Hot peppers
- Nectarines (imported)
- Peaches
- Potatoes
- Spinach

It's less important to buy these foods organic:

- Asparagus
- Avocados
- Cabbage
- Cantaloupe
- Corn
- Eggplant
- Grapefruit
- Kiwi
- Mangos
- Mushrooms

Other tips for reducing pesticide residue on your food: clean all fruits and vegetables well with water, and trim the fat from meat and chicken (pesticides build up in fatty tissue).

But feeding corn and soy to animals causes problems, too. For one thing, it's an inefficient use of energy, food, and water. Cows naturally graze in pastures, a process that usefully converts something humans can't eat (grass) into things we can eat (meat and milk). But every calorie of animal protein from meat takes 10 calories from plants to produce, whether the cow is fed grass or food like corn or soy, which people could eat. To think of it another way, the amount of food it takes to produce meat for 1 person could feed 10 people if it were eaten directly.

Also, cows have evolved to eat grass, not corn and soy—which are too rich for their stomachs. Eating them causes digestive problems and makes the cows sick. So they're given medicines and antibiotics, which can then end up in the meat humans eat. And their richer diet creates ideal stomach conditions for the growth of a particular strain of the dangerous E. coli bacteria, which can contaminate meat if proper procedures aren't followed during slaughtering. If the contaminated meat isn't cooked thoroughly, it can sicken or sometimes even kill people who eat it. Based on information like this, many people have chosen to go with grass-fed beef—which tends to contain more nutrients and healthier fat, and is easier on the environment. In 1998, there were only about 100 farmers raising grass-fed cows in the U.S., but today that number is in the thousands, and you can now find grass-fed beef at many grocery stores.

Madison Vorva and Rhiannon Tomtishen's campaign inspired nearly 70,000 protest e-mails to Girl Scouts USA.

FACING PALM

Turns out palm trees aren't just a nice backdrop for your next vacation selfie. The fruit from certain kinds of palms is used to produce a vegetable oil that stays solid at room temperature—making it a hot item for food manufacturers. Palm oil is used in hundreds of products, including crackers, margarine, baked goods, candies, and cosmetics and household products. Most palm oil is produced in Indonesia and Malaysia, where the demand for it is causing large areas of previously untouched rainforest and orangutan habitat to be cut down.

In 2007, when two 11-year-old Girl Scouts, Madison Vorva and Rhiannon Tomtishen, realized that the cookies they were selling contained palm oil that was linked to deforestation, they started a campaign to get Girl Scouts to stop using it, launching petitions and gaining support from environmental organizations. It took nearly five years, but Girl Scouts USA eventually took measures to reduce the impact of the palm oil they use, and the food company Kellogg's—which bakes some Girl Scout cookies—committed to using only sustainably produced palm oil. In 2012, the girls received an award from the United Nations in recognition of their campaign. Since then other activist groups have launched campaigns to get chains, including Krispy Kreme and Tim Hortons, to stop using non-sustainable palm oil.

GLOBAL EFFECTS

ALL THIS CHEAP, PLENTIFUL FOOD sounds like a good thing—after all, a smaller percentage of the world's population is starving or malnourished than ever before—but the effects of producing cheap crops like corn and soy can actually make food systems *less* secure.

How? Consider what happens when food intersects with the global economy. Traditionally, many countries have imposed tariffs, or limits on how much of a product can be imported. When a tariff on a certain type of food is in place, anyone shipping that food into the country has to pay an additional fee. The idea is to help protect local farmers who produce that food. But under international free trade agreements, most types of food from the U.S. and Canada can be imported to Mexico or Central American countries without paying tariffs.

Mexican workers weeding a field in California. Over 75 percent of U.S. farm workers come from Mexico or Central America, often after losing farms or jobs in their home countries.

Since U.S. and Canadian soybeans, wheat, and corn are grown on a large scale with financial assistance from the government, they're much cheaper than the crops produced by local farmers in those other countries.

So what happens to those local farmers? To survive, they are often encouraged to switch from growing food intended for local consumption to growing a crop meant for export to other countries. Families that have survived for generations by growing their own food and selling it to their neighbors have lost their land or are being forced to migrate to find new jobs because of lowered prices brought about by globalization.

MILES TO GO

EXPORTING AND IMPORTING FOOD is not only a concern for small-scale farmers and producers. All food takes energy to produce, as well as to transport to where it's sold. When that energy comes from fossil fuels like oil, it contributes to greenhouse gas emissions and climate change. Many people concerned about climate change have started thinking about food in terms of its "carbon footprint," or how much greenhouse gas is emitted as a result of getting food to your plate. One concept that's become popular is the idea of "food miles," which reflect how far your food has traveled to reach you. Followers of trends like the 100-mile diet believe we should choose food produced within a short distance from where we live.

SHRINKING YOUR FOOTPRINT

When it comes to getting food from farm to table, lamb, beef, cheese, pork, farmed salmon, turkey, and chicken top the list for greenhouse gas emissions. Where do those emissions come from? Partly from replacing forests with pasture, which releases CO_2 from the soil and removes trees that pull CO_2 from the air. It's also from animal waste, which is responsible for two-thirds of global emissions of nitrous oxide, a potent greenhouse gas. And cows are notorious for intestinal gas (yes, that kind of gas), which owes its distinctive odor to methane, another greenhouse gas. Feeding all those animals, preparing the product for the grocery shelf, and getting the packaged meat to market uses a lot of energy, too. So if you're looking to make a difference in the carbon footprint of your diet, try eating beef, milk, and cheese less often.

Buying local produce in season usually represents a better environmental choice (and often tastes better too). But it's not always so simple. For one thing, locally grown food often costs more. For another, transportation is actually only a small factor in a food's total carbon footprint. Growing, processing, and manufacturing accounts for a much bigger part of the overall energy used to get food from the farm to your table.

Working out the environmental impact of a particular food can be incredibly complicated. Think of even one vegetable or piece of fruit: What growing methods were used—was it grown outside, or in a heated greenhouse? Were machines used to plant and harvest it, or human labor? How was it stored? Did it have to be cooked or otherwise processed before reaching you? At what time of year was it grown?

Here's an example: in North America, apples are normally harvested in the fall. It makes sense to eat local apples when they're in season. But by the following summer, those apples have been kept in storage for so long that the energy required to keep them cold and fresh exceeds the energy it requires to ship apples from New Zealand, where they're in season. Choosing local apples that have been in storage all year doesn't have an environmental advantage. All that just for an apple. Now try figuring out the carbon footprint of a pizza with a dozen different toppings, or a can of vegetable soup with 20 or more ingredients!

LIVING LIKE ANIMALS

THE WORD "FARM" might bring to mind an idyllic image of a cow grazing in a field of grass, or a chicken happily pecking around in a henhouse. But that picture no longer represents reality for the vast majority of the meat, milk, and eggs found in supermarkets today. Those products usually come from animals raised in "factory farms." These farms do a few things well: they produce big volumes of meat, dairy, and eggs, and they've brought down the cost of products that used to be too expensive for many people to afford regularly. However, this cheap and plentiful production comes with a cost.

We know from biologists that animals feel pain, experience stress and fear, and have a variety of physical and psychological needs, from the need to root around in the dirt to the need to interact with other animals. Pigs are considered to be at least as smart as dogs and have personalities as distinct. Cows have been shown to develop "friendships" with each other, and feel stress when they're separated.

Even chickens develop complex social structures and have more than 30 different types of calls that they use to communicate.

In the modern factory farm system, these animals are raised with the goal of maximizing output and minimizing costs. Animals in factory farms are often kept in crowded conditions that deny the animals' natural instincts and needs. Cows are packed together by the thousands in feedlots, fattening up on a diet of corn and soy, while dairy cows are regularly impregnated so they keep producing milk. They often develop painful inflammations of their udders due to unsanitary conditions. The grim facts are that 9 out of 10 sows (female pigs) in the U.S. are raised in gestation crates—concrete stalls so small that they can't turn around. Sadly, the majority of chickens raised for food spend their entire lives in sheds with tens of thousands of other birds, never seeing the sun or breathing fresh air. Hens raised to lay eggs are kept in wire cages too small to spread their wings.

Chicks are kept in an incubator before being transferred to cages or sheds.

KINDER CUTS

There is good news for animals raised for food:

✳ Many farmers have always made animal welfare a priority, and more are getting on board every day. Niman Ranch, for instance, is a network of 500 U.S. farmers committed to raising pigs humanely. Farmers even hire animal psychologists to help develop ways to raise and slaughter animals without causing them too much stress.

✳ A number of companies, under pressure from consumers and animal welfare organizations, have refused to use meat or eggs produced using troubling practices. Chipotle, Burger King, McDonald's, Safeway, and Costco, for example, have agreed not to use pigs kept in gestation crates. When these big companies set rules, their suppliers must follow suit, leading to more humane practices all along the chain.

✳ Consumer demand for things like free-range chickens, cage-free eggs, and pasture-raised beef keeps going up. And more information often leads to kinder choices. When a grocery store in Vancouver, B.C., labeled cartons of different kinds of eggs with explanations of how the chickens were raised, sales of organic eggs—which have the highest animal welfare standards—went up the most.

In the U.S., 7 billion chickens are killed for food each year—about 22 chickens for every person in the country. That's a lot of nuggets!

THE ARMS RACE

Livestock farms are a major source of superbugs—strong strains of bacteria that develop in response to antibiotics, which are routinely given to animals not only to treat illness but also to help them grow. The trouble is that some bacteria genes manage to survive antibiotic treatment. They then evolve to create stronger strains of bacteria, requiring more potent antibiotics or larger doses to destroy them—creating a kind of arms race between antibiotics and bacteria.

Superbugs that develop around animals can jump to humans, usually farm workers. As meat demand is increasing in China and India, and factory farming techniques are becoming more common there, the overuse of antibiotics in animals has been blamed for deadly viruses like the swine flu, which killed an estimated 284,500 people worldwide in a 2009 outbreak.

In Europe, antibiotics can now only be used to treat sick animals, and some grocery stores in North America refuse to carry meat that has been produced using antibiotics.

Around 80 percent of the antibiotics supply in the U.S. is administered to animals.

WELFARE STATE

THE TRANSPORT TO SLAUGHTERHOUSES can be hard on animals, too. They're often placed in crowded trucks, exposed to extreme temperatures, and sometimes go days without food or water. Millions die this way every year, and even more become injured or sick.

States and provinces all have laws to prevent animals from being abused, but those that apply to livestock animals are often not very strict, or are weakly enforced. Animal welfare organizations have revealed many disturbing incidents in factory farms and slaughter-houses. But instead of improving the conditions, powerful lobbyists for the agriculture industry have supported "anti-whistleblower" bills in dozens of states that would make it illegal to expose mistreatment of animals in farms and slaughterhouses. (Lobbyists are people who are paid to speak to politicians on behalf of a particular group.) As of 2014, none of these bills have passed.

INFOBITES
MEATONOMICS

AVERAGE U.S. PRICE OF HALF A KILOGRAM (1 LB) OF CHICKEN:

1935 (inflation adjusted): **$5.07**   Today: **$1.34**

AMOUNT OF CHICKEN CONSUMED BY AVERAGE AMERICAN PER YEAR:

1935:
4 kg
(9 lbs)

Today:
25.4 kg
(56 lbs)

AMOUNT OF MILK PRODUCED IN THE U.S. PER YEAR:

1950s
(14 billion gallons)

53 billion liters

87 billion liters

Today
(23 billion gallons)

AMOUNT OF MILK PRODUCED PER COW PER YEAR:

1950s
2,400 liters
(634 gallons)

Today
6,700 liters
(1,770 gallons)

The realities of factory farms and slaughterhouses are not pleasant, and it's tempting to blame farmers, workers, or slaughterhouse owners. But it's important to remember that most of these people aren't trying to make animals suffer; they're merely doing their jobs. Responsibility also lies with consumers, and that includes all of us who create the demand for high volumes of cheap animal products. One way you can help change things is to make meat go further—for example, by eating meat only a few times a week, or using smaller amounts in a stir-fry or stew.

MEATLESS MILLIONS

Many people around the world don't eat meat at all. Some belong to religious traditions, like Hinduism or Buddhism, that teach it's wrong to harm any living creature. Some don't believe in keeping animals in confinement, and choose to boycott the products of a system they see as inhumane. Others choose to be vegetarian to reduce their impact on the environment, or for health reasons.

"Flexible vegetarianism" is becoming a popular option too. Movements like Meatless Mondays and the VB6 diet—which involves eating only plant foods before 6 p.m.—have spawned cookbooks, websites, and social media campaigns. If you don't want to completely give up meat but are concerned about the effect of eating a lot of it, these flexible approaches can be good options.

GOING TO THE FISH FARM

WHEN YOU TAKE A CLOSER LOOK at how animals are raised on a factory farm, fish might seem like a more humane and environmentally friendly alternative.

Fishing has been a part of human culture for at least 40,000 years; almost every group of humans living near water has found some way to catch and eat fish, shellfish, squid, and even mammals like seals and whales. Traditional cultures often devised ingenious ways to catch fish, like hand catching, netting, spearing, or setting traps. Fishing canoes and rafts date back at least 7,000 years, and the ancient Egyptians and Scandinavians built large fishing boats with sails. Some cultures also raised fish in captivity for food: indigenous Australians raised eels in a complex lake channel system as long ago as 6000 BCE, and around 2500 BCE the Chinese were trapping carp in lakes and feeding them. The ancient Romans also bred fish in ponds.

Today, about a third of the fish and seafood sold for food in North America is raised in modern versions of these ancient "aquaculture" environments. Fish are raised in large tanks, natural or human-made ponds, or enclosed cages in oceans, lakes, or rivers. Done right, aquaculture is a good thing: it can be sustainable, and can help reduce the impact of fishing on the ocean.

However, some aquaculture environments are essentially underwater factory farms, complete with hundreds of thousands of fish crammed into cages where waste builds up, and fish are subject to injury. Not surprisingly, these conditions breed problems—and parasites! Sea lice, which proliferate at a rate 30,000 times higher in farms than they do in the open ocean, are particularly nasty critters that eat away at salmon and other fish, creating deep wounds and sometimes killing them. The lice have even spread to salmon in the wild.

PLENTY OF FISH IN THE SEA?

IF YOU EAT A WILD FISH, you can at least rest assured that it hasn't spent its whole life in a crowded cage. But sadly, the methods used to catch the majority of wild fish are having devastating effects on our oceans.

Fishing is a huge industry, employing around 200 million people around the world, and fish and seafood are a main source of protein for about one in five people globally. At one time, people thought the ocean's resources could feed a growing population forever. Today, we know that's not true. Overfishing is threatening both the health of the ocean and the food supply. Experts estimate that around 90 percent of all large predatory fish (like tuna, swordfish, and sharks) have already disappeared.

Bycatch from fishing nets can include large fish, like this young shark.

How are all of these fish being caught? The most common practice is longlines, some stretching as far as 100 kilometers (62 miles) behind fishing boats with thousands of baited hooks attached. Fish such as tuna and herring are usually caught by purse seines, giant nets that encircle schools of fish and are drawn together tightly at the top. Then there's trawling, where shrimp and other types of fish are caught by an immense, funnel-shaped net that's dragged behind a boat.

These methods all have one thing in common: along with the fish being caught, other species—such as sharks, sea turtles, dolphins, whales, marlins, and even some sea birds, like albatross, as well as "trash fish" that are considered too small or not tasty enough to eat—are gathered up. The undesired animals, known as "bycatch," are thrown overboard, many of them injured or already dead. Millions of sea animals die this way every year, about 25 percent of the total worldwide catch.

Bottom trawling, where a net is dragged along the ocean floor, is the worst offender—on average, 80 to 90 percent of a trawling net's catch is thrown back. This practice greatly reduces the diversity of ocean life, destroying ecosystems and leading to endangerment of some species.

WISE CHOICES

So farmed fish has its downsides, wild fish has its downsides—what's left to eat? There are ways of fishing that focus on abundant species, and use methods that limit bycatch and damage to underwater habitats. Hook and line fishing, trolling (drawing baited fishing lines through the water behind a boat), and trapping are usually considered more sustainable ways to fish. Programs like Ocean Wise and SeaChoice provide lists of the most and least sustainable wild and farmed seafoods. Some restaurants, food stores, and fish markets have partnered with these programs and show symbols on their menus or signs to indicate sustainable seafood options. You can help by watching for these symbols and choosing sustainable seafood options for home or in a restaurant.

A large net full of fish is hauled up onto the deck of a trawler.

Can we turn trash into treasure? The David Suzuki Foundation has launched a campaign to persuade people to eat spiny dogfish—small sharks that, despite being abundant and tasty, are usually thrown out by fisheries as "trash." Eating more of these kinds of fish (or other small, plentiful fish like sardines) helps reduce the demand for overfished species like halibut, cod, or tuna.

WASTE NOT, WANT NOT

THE WORLD PRODUCES A LOT OF FOOD to feed a growing population. And yet, nearly a third of the global food supply—about 1.3 billion metric tons of food—goes to waste every year, spoiled during transport or processing, or thrown away in stores, restaurants, or homes. That's enough to feed over 2 billion people! About 40 percent of all food produced in North America is thrown away.

How can we reduce the amount of food wasted in our homes? We can start by planning meals before shopping, buying smaller amounts of food more often, and storing food properly so it doesn't spoil quickly (for instance, take fruits and vegetables out of plastic bags, and don't wash them until you're going to eat them). And if you have backyard space or a local program, compost food scraps instead of throwing them away.

Technology can also help prevent waste: scientists have tested a computer chip that can be inserted in packages of perishable food and will send a text to your phone when it detects the food is approaching its expiry date!

Grocery stores and restaurants throw away a lot of food that might be a few days old, or maybe doesn't look as perfect as a customer might want it to look. But many owners, as well as food wholesalers, corporations, and caterers, reduce waste by donating those "extras" to food banks. It's a brilliant way of feeding hungry families and reducing waste at the same time.

People who call themselves "freegans" take the anti-waste philosophy to an extreme by salvaging food that's in edible condition from garbage bins behind grocery stores and restaurants. It's a cheap way to dine out, but not necessarily hygienic!

FOOD FOR THOUGHT

What can you do to make sure you're making the best food choices that are the least harmful to the environment? You can't very well stop eating until the "perfect" option comes along, one that was manufactured without any bad effects. But here are a few small, but important steps you can take:

Try to add one food, or source of food, that comes from outside the "big" food system, whether that means starting a veggie garden in your yard, visiting a local farm stand or farmers' market once a month, or planting a small herb garden in a pot on your windowsill.

Try replacing one less-than-healthy corn- or soy-containing food in your diet with a healthier alternative: for instance, eating oatmeal and fruit for breakfast instead of a sugary corn-based cereal, or drinking homemade iced tea instead of soft drinks containing high-fructose corn syrup.

If your family eats meat, discuss ways to reduce the amount you eat, whether by taking part in Meatless Mondays (you can find lots of support and meatless recipes online) or eating meat as an accent rather than the main part of a dish. If you cut out meat, make sure to substitute with foods containing protein and iron, like chickpeas, beans, veggie meat substitutes, or nuts.

CHAPTER 3

GOOD FOR YOU

"**L**ET FOOD BE YOUR MEDICINE, and medicine be your food,"
said Hippocrates, a famous doctor in ancient Greece. His advice
says a lot about how deeply food is connected to our health.
Have you ever eaten too much junk at lunch, and had no energy in the
afternoon? Or gotten a boost from a great breakfast or fruit smoothie?
If food can affect us this way in only a few hours or a day, imagine how
our eating habits can affect our bodies after weeks, months, or years.

News reports and public health experts talk about an obesity crisis
in North America. They hammer home the message that we eat too
much sugar, unhealthy fats, salt, and processed foods, and not enough
vegetables and fruits. Many North Americans don't even have easy

access to basic fresh, healthy foods, while others spend countless hours discussing diets—low-carb, high-protein, vegan, gluten-free—that you practically need a degree in nutrition to understand. What's going on?

The messages we get about food and nutrition can be confusing, and are often contradictory. Even nutrition experts don't always agree about what's actually good for you. So, what do we really know about food and health?

NUTRITION 101

YOU PROBABLY LEARNED the basics of nutrition back in grade school, but here's a quick refresher: food contains calories, which is another way of saying energy, and our bodies need energy to survive. When we eat, our bodies break the food down and use its energy to do all the things bodies do, like moving, thinking, keeping our organs running, and making new cells and blood. If we use up more energy than we take in, our bodies digest their own fat, and then their muscles. If we eat more calories than we use, our bodies store the extra energy as fat.

Food has three basic building blocks: protein, carbohydrates (or carbs), and fat. Protein is made up of amino acids and is found in food that comes from animals—meat, fish, milk, and eggs—as well as in beans, nuts, and seeds. We need it to keep our muscles, internal organs, hair, and skin healthy and growing, and to form blood cells. Though our bodies make some amino acids, we need to get others—called essential amino acids—from food. Food that comes from animals has all the essential amino acids, but most plant proteins only have certain ones, so you have to eat a variety of foods to get the complete set.

Carbs, which come from starchy foods like bread, grains, and potatoes, as well as vegetables and fruits, give us the energy we need to move. But there are different kinds of carbs, and they affect our bodies in different ways. A doughnut has one kind, and a salad made with tomatoes, carrots, and chickpeas has another. What's the difference? "Complex" carbs such as whole wheat bread, brown rice, fruits, vegetables, and beans have lots of fiber and nutrients. They take longer for our bodies to break down, and so give us energy over a longer time. "Simple" carbs are things like white bread and rice, cakes, cookies, and anything containing sugar as an added ingredient (as opposed to the sugar that's a natural part of fruit). They usually don't have much fiber or many nutrients, which are stripped away when whole grains like wheat are refined to make white flour. Our bodies break down simple carbs very quickly, which makes our blood sugar levels rise. That makes them great when we need a fast burst of energy, or sugar rush. But soon after, your blood sugar levels drop again—a sugar crash.

JUST DESSERTS

BEFORE WE GET TO THE THIRD building block of food, let's take a detour to explore everyone's favorite simple carb: sugar.

Sugar is the taste of happiness, and that's not just an expression: when you eat it, it raises the "reward chemical," dopamine, in your brain, which gives you that jolt of pleasure similar to when you win a soccer game, or get a great mark on your art project. It also makes our bodies produce serotonin, a hormone that makes us feel nicely relaxed and comforted. Our happy associations with sugar don't end there—it's social, too. Sugar is part of almost every celebration or big event in our lives. What would birthdays be without cake, Halloween without candy, or Valentine's Day without chocolate? From the time we're kids, we look forward to ice cream cones on a summer evening or hot chocolate after ice-skating. No wonder sugar is so alluring.

Unfortunately, sugar is one of the worst things we can eat—though that's not stopping us from eating it. Americans consume about 35 kilograms (77 pounds) of added sugar every year, and Canadians pack away even more. For a long time, nutritionists considered sugar to be empty calories, and dentists have never been fans of the stuff. But research now shows that eating too much sugar could be even worse than we thought.

want to avoid added sugar? You'll have to be a food label detective, because it goes under many aliases. Some ingredients to check for: sucrose, dextrose, glucose, fructose, honey, cane juice, fruit juice concentrate, barley malt, caramel, any kind of syrup, and, of course, sugar.

SWEET AND LOW

SO WHAT EXACTLY HAPPENS WHEN YOU EAT SUGAR? At first it produces that oh-so-pleasant dopamine and serotonin rush, but the feeling doesn't last long. Eat too much added sugar and it starts to mess with the natural dopamine levels in your brain. You start to feel irritated and tired, and you can even get a kind of "brain fog" that makes it hard to remember things or think clearly. Your body craves more sugar to get that dopamine rush again, and before you know it, you need even more of the stuff to re-create the "high." It's no wonder some researchers think sugar is an addictive substance, much like alcohol or drugs.

Then there's sugar's effect on your liver. Chemically, white sugar is about half glucose and half fructose. When we eat too much fructose (in forms like soft drinks and candy, rather than fruit, which is processed more slowly), our livers can't deal with all of it, so they convert it to fat, and send some into our blood. Over time, this increases a person's blood pressure and risk of type 2 diabetes.

People with diabetes need to monitor their blood glucose levels regularly.

If you're thinking, "But I'm a teenager! I don't have to worry about that," hold on a moment. While it's true that people usually develop these conditions as adults (due to the usual culprits—bad diets, lack of exercise, and excess weight), rates of type 2 diabetes among kids and teens shot up by 30 percent between 2000 and 2009. The frightening truth is that tens of thousands of kids in North America now suffer from it, and even more—about one in four teens in the U.S.—are considered pre-diabetic, which means their blood sugar levels are so high that one day they're likely to develop diabetes. Of course those teens also have a much higher risk of developing other serious health problems later on.

The World Health Organization recommends no more than 5 teaspoons of added sugar per day. To put that into perspective, a can of soda has about 10 teaspoons of sugar. The average American consumes a whopping 22 teaspoons a day, and Canadians 26. That's a whole lot of sugar!

SUGAR BUSTERS

Breaking the sugar habit can be hard—and you have to admit that life wouldn't be much fun without a piece of chocolate or an ice cream cone now and again. Even so, it's best to avoid going overboard. Here are a few tips to keep the sugar you eat in check:

* Control the amount of added sugar you take in from processed food. Try plain versions of foods like yogurt or oatmeal, and add your own fruit or a touch of honey.

* If you're baking cookies, a cake, or muffins, reduce the amount of sugar in the recipe by a quarter to a third. Chances are you won't even notice!

* Sweetened drinks, and even fruit juices, are instant sugar-delivery systems with little nutritional benefit. Think of them as occasional treats, and drink water instead.

* Watch out for "secretly" sweet foods like ketchup and salad dressing. Make your own (you can find easy recipes with just a few ingredients) or check labels and buy ones with less added sugar.

SWEET PURSUITS

Are our bodies built to handle sugar in its modern form? Many nutritionists don't think so. Early humans didn't encounter concentrated sources of sugar, like soft drinks and chocolate bars, and even sweet fruit was so hard to find that their bodies responded by storing its precious sugar as fat. That would have been helpful in the prehistoric age when food was sometimes scarce, but not now.

Only a few centuries ago, sugar was a rare and expensive luxury. In the 18th and 19th centuries, Europeans' taste for it led them to develop huge sugar plantations on Caribbean islands to satisfy their demand. Of the more than 11 million Africans sent as slaves to the New World, over half ended up working on sugar plantations. Eventually sugar became more widely available and the price went down.

Today, sugar (or one of its variants) is in nearly every processed food we eat. Even things you wouldn't think of as sweet, like fast-food hamburgers, tomato-based sauces, and peanut butter, have added sugar. Considering our bodies evolved to run on very small amounts of sweet stuff, that's a lot of sugar to take in!

FAT FACTS

NOW, BACK TO THE LAST building block of food: fats, which we get from meat, dairy, eggs, fish, nuts, avocados, and vegetable oils. These fats can be our friends—they help us absorb vitamins, keep our joints and heart healthy, help our immune systems fight illness, and even make our skin soft and hair shiny. Like carbs, fats come in a few different forms, some healthier than others.

Vegetable oils (like olive, safflower, and canola), as well as fish, nuts, and seeds, contain fats that keep your heart healthy by raising "good" cholesterol—the kind that doesn't build up in your arteries. These fats are usually liquid at room temperature. Saturated fat, found in meat and dairy, and in coconut and palm oil, is usually solid at room temperature (think of butter). For a long time it was believed to raise "bad" cholesterol, the kind that does build up in your arteries and increases your risk of heart disease and diabetes. But some nutritionists and

doctors have begun to question whether saturated fats are really so bad. Some studies have shown that cutting out these fats doesn't have any effect on cholesterol levels or heart disease.

There's no controversy about trans fats, the bad guys on the block.

Everyone agrees you should steer clear. Created when vegetable oils are "saturated" with hydrogen atoms, making them solid, they're often used in margarine, cookies, crackers, and baked goods to give them the right consistency and make them last longer on the shelf. Many fast-food restaurants use them for deep-frying, too. Trans fats became popular as a replacement for more expensive solid fats like butter, lard, and palm oil, and, remarkably, at one time they were even considered healthier. But studies in the 1990s started to show that trans fats raise "bad" cholesterol and lead to heart disease, and they've even been banned in many countries.

Want to find out how your food stacks up nutritionally? Google provides an instant nutrient analysis on the right side of the results page when you search for any food. You can also compare different foods: simply type "compare broccoli and chocolate milk" (or whatever you want to look up) in the search bar, hit enter, and the nutrient profiles will pop up side by side.

PROTEIN SOURCES

In North America, when we think "protein" we usually think "meat." But around the world, as many as 1 in 20 people don't eat meat, and for many more it's only an occasional food. In the U.S., about 3 percent of people call themselves vegetarian.

Vegetarianism goes back thousands of years to ancient India and Greece, where it was connected to the belief that animals shouldn't be harmed. Throughout history there have been vegetarian movements and groups, from Buddhists in Japan to European artists in the Renaissance era to Christian groups in the colonial U.S.

Today, vegetarians give many different reasons for their choice of diet, including concerns about the treatment of animals, the environment, and their health. The major health argument for vegetarianism is that meat is high in saturated fat and cholesterol, which are linked to heart problems and colon cancer. Vegetarians do have lower rates of heart disease, certain cancers, diabetes, and obesity, and the rates for vegans, who avoid dairy products and eggs as well as meat and fish, are even lower.

Vegetarian and vegan diets can be very healthy. But cutting out animal products without all the facts is unlikely to lead to good nutrition or a diet you can stick with, and vegetarians who eat mostly cheese pizza, French fries, and doughnuts won't stay healthy. Foods high in protein and iron, like beans, whole grains, nuts, seeds, and meat substitutes, are critical to the vegetarian and vegan diet.

INFOBITES
SUGAR THROUGH HISTORY

AVERAGE AMOUNT OF ADDED SUGAR CONSUMED PER PERSON PER YEAR:

England, 1700: 1.8 kg (4 lbs)

England, 1800: 8 kg (18 lbs)

England, 1870: 21 kg (47 lbs)

England, 1900: 45 kg (100 lbs)

U.S., today: 59 kg (130 lbs)

France, today: 40 kg (88 lbs)

Japan, today: 31 kg (68 lbs)

SUGAR AND TEENS

AVERAGE AMOUNT OF ADDED SUGAR TEENS IN THE U.S. CONSUME PER DAY:

34 tsp

(Recommended amount: 5 tsp)

HOW MUCH ADDED SUGAR IS IN A ...

81 g (19 tsp) — 590 mL (20 oz) Starbucks Caramel Frappuccino

77 g (18 tsp) — 590 mL (20 oz) bottle of Mountain Dew

39 g (9 tsp) — 355 mL (12 oz) can of Coca-Cola

THAT SANDWICH IS SO OVER

Our bodies need protein, carbs, and fat to work properly. But over the years, these building blocks have gone in and out of fashion, much like clothing styles. In the 1970s and '80s, high-protein, high-fat, low-carb diets were all the rage, and dieters were advised to eat things like steaks with a pat of butter on top, or raw-egg shakes. Then, fat got a bad reputation (carbs were okay, though), and before you knew it, grocery stores were stocking all sorts of fat-free cookies, snacks, and frozen dinners. In the 2000s, food fashion changed yet again and diet doctors were soon promoting extremely low-carb, high-protein diets based around meat and salad. It's hard to keep up with such wild swings in what we're told is healthy eating.

Through all the changing fads, many doctors and nutrition experts have advised a balanced approach, combining healthy carbs (like vegetables, fruit, whole grains, and beans) and healthy fats (like nuts and olive oil) with smaller amounts of meat, dairy, and processed carbs.

When you think a food sounds healthy—say low-fat ice cream, or organic chips—chances are you'll eat more of it. This tendency is so common it has a name: the Snackwell Effect, after a low-fat cookie brand. It doesn't just go for food, either: people tend to use energy-efficient washing machines more often, and leave low-power lightbulbs on longer than regular ones.

METABOLIZE THIS

SO, EAT MORE FOOD AND YOU GAIN WEIGHT, eat less food and you lose it, right? Thanks to metabolism—the process in your body that converts food to energy—it's not quite that simple. Just like different models of cars, some bodies burn fuel faster than others. The speed at which your body does this is influenced by a lot of things: your age (older people tend to burn fewer calories than younger ones), body size (people who are bigger or have more muscle burn more calories, even when they're resting), and how active you are.

Metabolism is also influenced by evolution. We evolved to survive during periods when food was scarce, like the winter months. Our metabolic systems are very smart: when we don't have much food to eat, they slow down and conserve calories until our next meal comes along. That's why people on diets, or who skip meals, sometimes stop losing weight, or gain it back very quickly once they start eating normally—their bodies think they're starving, and a starving body tries to hang onto calories to survive. Eating small meals or snacking often through the day is a good way to keep your metabolism running high, as is getting enough exercise.

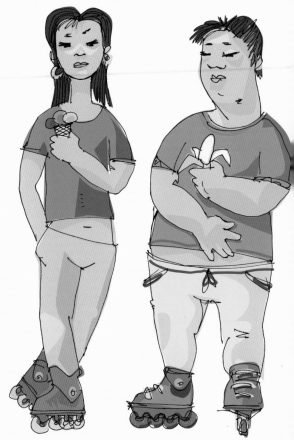

DOWN THE ROAD

N THE 2004 DOCUMENTARY *Super Size Me*, filmmaker Morgan Spurlock conducted an unusual experiment: he wanted to see what would happen if he ate nothing but McDonald's food three times a day for a whole month. The results were dramatic: after less than two weeks on his 5,000-calorie-a-day, all-cheeseburger, fries, and milkshake diet, the previously healthy Spurlock had gained weight and was experiencing major mood swings, headaches, loss of energy, and heart palpitations. By the end of the experiment, he had gained 11 kilograms (almost 25 pounds), his cholesterol levels had shot up, and his doctors were astonished at how rapidly his health had gone downhill.

Spurlock's experiment was a shocking example of how quickly a bad diet can have a big effect on your health. But it's also an extreme—most of us don't eat a full fast-food meal three times a day, or force ourselves to eat twice as many calories as we need in order to make an exciting movie. So what happens to your body if you eat greasy burgers, fries, and shakes, say, twice a week, or once a month? Unfortunately, no one has made that documentary yet, so it's hard to say.

One reason it can be hard to know what exactly makes up a healthy diet is that most of the time, food affects our bodies over the long term. If you eat food that's spoiled, or a food you're allergic to, you'll have a reaction right away. But normally, the effect isn't quite so obvious, or sudden. And because most of us eat lots of different foods, and there are all sorts of other things

that influence our health—like our genetics or environment, or how much we exercise—it can be hard to pinpoint how a particular food or even our daily eating habits are affecting our health.

There's also the fact that people's bodies are unique, and respond to foods in different ways. Most of us know some lucky person who seems to survive only on junk food, yet stays thin and apparently healthy. Then there are people who conscientiously eat salads and brown rice and never touch processed food, yet get sick all the time. But even though there are exceptions, eating a generally healthy diet—meaning lots of vegetables, fruits, and whole foods, and not too much processed food or sugar—will usually help you feel better and stay healthier.

MUD PIE, ANYONE?

When we don't get the vitamins and minerals we need, our bodies can compensate in some pretty unusual ways. Pica is a medical condition that occurs when people have a compulsion to eat things that aren't food, like dirt, chalk, or clay. Sounds like a strange addiction out of a reality TV show, but it's fairly common in kids and pregnant women. It may be caused by nutrient deficiency—someone whose body is low on iron or calcium, for example, might develop an intense craving for a mineral-rich substance like clay or dirt. Pregnant women in India have even been known to suck on limestone, a rock containing calcium, which helps to build bones.

WARNING: THIS PARAGRAPH CONTAINS PEANUTS

ALLERGIES ARE AN EXTREME EXAMPLE of just how different individual reactions to the same food can be. Sometimes your body's immune system mistakes a protein in food for something harmful—no one knows exactly why. When this happens, your immune system sends white blood cells to attack the imagined invader, producing an allergic "reaction"—anything from a skin rash or a funny feeling in the mouth to trouble breathing and even a life-threatening reaction called anaphylaxis. Even a tiny amount of the substance can sometimes be enough to trigger a reaction. For sufferers, allergies can cause a lot of inconvenience and worry. Some kids do outgrow allergies as they get older, but there's no known cure.

Food allergies have become much more common in Western countries over the last few decades, for reasons that aren't completely

understood. At least 1 in 20 North American kids under three years old are thought to have a food allergy, and doctors report an increase in emergency room visits for allergic reactions. Food companies must now identify potential allergens on their labels, and many schools have banned common allergens—like peanut butter—to prevent allergic kids from being exposed.

Meanwhile, in developing countries, allergies are much less common. Why the difference? The leading theory is that the Western world's overly clean modern lifestyles and diets are to blame. Turns out we may need some exposure to dirt and germs for our immune systems to develop properly, and for our guts to acquire the helpful bacteria that help us digest food.

There are other possible factors for the rise in allergies; everything from diet to lack of sunshine has been blamed. For now, all we really know is that we don't know enough about allergies!

Even people without allergies can be intolerant of certain foods—like lactose (the sugar in milk) or gluten (a protein found in wheat)—which means their bodies don't digest those substances properly. Food intolerances and sensitivities aren't always well understood because symptoms like bloating, tiredness, or headaches can be caused by any number of things. If it's diet, it can be hard to pin down exactly which ingredient or component is causing the problem. Still, many people find they feel better if they avoid certain foods, even if doctors don't yet know enough to explain why.

Over 90 percent of allergic reactions are caused by only eight foods: peanuts, other nuts, milk, fish, shellfish, eggs, soy, and wheat.

STUDIES SAY...

SO THE BIG QUESTION IS "How do we know what we should eat to stay healthy?" If you've ever seen the results of studies around nutrition reported online or on TV, you might have noticed that they sometimes contradict each other. Part of the reason is that nutrition, like any science, is always evolving, and scientists' understanding of it changes with new research and knowledge. Another problem is that studies often look at different elements of foods. One study, for example, might find that the fats in certain types of fish are good for you. A second study might show that mercury in fish is bad for you. When we hear the results reported, it may seem that scientists can't decide if fish is good or bad. And media stories often focus on a single study rather than comparing the results of a number of studies, which might have resulted in different conclusions.

Some studies fail to prove cause and effect. Maybe the results observe that eating a particular food is linked to a lower or higher risk of disease or weight gain. But what else is involved? For instance, a (purely imaginary) study might show that people who eat a lot of turnips are more likely to die in their sleep. It might turn out, however, that turnips don't actually *cause* people to die in their sleep, but that elderly people eat more turnips, and elderly people are more likely to die in their sleep.

And then there's the human challenge. People generally don't like being kept in a lab environment for months or years, so in order to gather information over the long term, studies often rely on food diaries. But people aren't so good at carefully following prescribed diets, or at accurately reporting what they ate, whether it's because they don't remember, didn't weigh or measure their food, or just don't want to admit they ate a whole pint of ice cream for breakfast.

Follow the money! Food companies pour lots of dollars into nutrition research, even sponsoring university departments (of nutrition, medicine, or agriculture), academic journals, and conferences for nutritionists. They often send out free samples and teaching materials to doctors, nutritionists, or professors. Do you think that kind of sponsorship can affect the results of these people's work?

SPONSORED BY...

OT ALL NUTRITION ADVICE comes from scientists or doctors; some comes from people who want us to eat more of a certain food.

Online articles and videos, and magazine columns, sometimes look like advice from a nutritionist. But the small print alongside the article (sometimes you have to look hard to find it!) might reveal that it's been produced and paid for by an organization representing some part of the food business, like dairy farmers or agriculture. That doesn't necessarily mean the advice isn't good, but if you know it's a marketing message in disguise, you might view it slightly differently.

In the U.S., nutrition advice in schools and doctors' offices is based on MyPlate (which replaced the previous Food Guide Pyramids); in Canada, the Food Guide is the go-to source for information. Both recommend how much of certain food groups (vegetables and fruit, grains, milk and alternatives, and meat and alternatives) we should eat every day. The food guides certainly provide positive advice—like making fruits and vegetables about half of your diet—but you still have to think carefully about what you're reading.

The food guides in Canada and the U.S. are created based on advice from scientists and nutrition experts, and they're presented to the public as objective, sound health guidelines. What's not usually revealed is that they're also shaped by the food industry. (An example: in 1992, when Canada's Food Guide was revised, both the meat and dairy industries complained that the recommended number of servings in the proposed version was too few, and the number was increased in the final guide.) Governments have obligations to protect their country's food producers *and* the health of their citizens, and those two goals can sometimes conflict. Both MyPlate and the Food Guide have been criticized by medical groups for promoting the interests of the dairy, meat, and grain industries. Dairy, for instance, is treated as its own separate food group even though many nutritionists argue it's not the only or best source of calcium. The recommendations also tend to be biased toward foods traditionally eaten by Caucasians. An estimated 50 million people in the U.S.—including a high proportion of Asian Americans, Native Americans, and African Americans—have trouble digesting the lactose in milk.

There are alternative guides to eating, developed by independent scientists without political pressure or influence from food industry groups. For instance, the Harvard School of Public Health's Healthy Eating Plate has some similarities to MyPlate, but puts more emphasis on vegetables, fish and vegetarian protein sources, and healthy fats, and doesn't consider dairy a main food group.

Eat more! No, eat less! Until pretty recently, most North American food advice focused on getting people to pack in more calories. That's because during times of scarcity, like the Great Depression and the world wars, people were likely to suffer from undernourishment and diseases caused by vitamin deficiencies (like scurvy or rickets). Today that has flipped and over-nourishment is seen as the bigger problem.

DO YOUR DUTY— EAT LOBSTER!

Government food guides have always had a history of political overtones: in Canada, the first Official Food Rules guide, published in 1942, was partly aimed at promoting the military effort in World War II and encouraging strong workers at home. Federal programs discouraged consumption of foods that were needed for export to soldiers overseas (like meat, butter, tea, and sugar), and encouraged Canadians to eat foods like lobster that couldn't be exported. The food guide featured slogans like "Canada needs you strong," and beside the recommendation for how much dairy to consume, there's an illustration of a milk bottle holding a rifle. A U.S. government food guide from the same era also presents nutrition as a patriotic duty, urging citizens to eat food from each of the "basic 7" groups every day (among them the "oranges, tomatoes, and grapefruit" group and the "butter and fortified margarine" group) because the "U.S. needs us strong."

MILLIONS OF UNSATISFIED CUSTOMERS

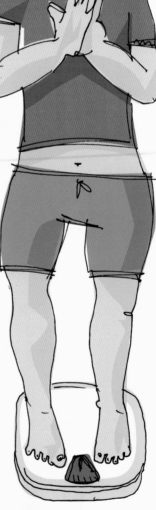

GOODBYE BELLY FAT! *Lose 39 pounds fast! Amazing weight loss, incredible energy!* You can barely turn your head without coming across appeals from the diet industry, which in North America is worth over a whopping $70 billion per year. Countless diet books and cookbooks, videos, meals, and supplements are sold every year, all aimed at helping people lose weight or get healthier. Yet more and more people in North America suffer from diet-related health problems, and rising obesity rates are a major concern. Why is that?

In American culture, thinner bodies tend to be valued over larger ones: the women who are presented as attractive in the media tend to be thin—often extremely so—and guys are usually muscular and toned. So it's no surprise that a lot of food and diet advice emphasizes losing weight or attaining a certain body shape, instead of being healthy. In fact, you can't always judge someone's health by their looks. A person who would be classified as overweight according to doctors' charts might be able to run marathons, while the model depicted as the picture of health on the cover of a fitness magazine might be ready to drop from hunger.

About half of teenage girls in the U.S. and a quarter of boys have tried dieting to lose weight, and might be attracted to ads promising they'll lose 10 pounds in a month by taking a supplement, or get a perfect body and glowing skin by following a certain diet plan. Most diets will lead to some weight loss—especially at the beginning—but it's hard to keep up a restrictive diet over a long period of time. It's a sad fact that despite their best efforts, about 8 in 10 people who have lost weight on a diet end up gaining it back.

Many people want a quick, easy answer. Unfortunately, eating balanced meals and healthy snacks, exercising, and avoiding sugar and junk food sounds boring, and it might take months to see results. But in the long run, this sensible, healthy approach is usually more effective than the newest diet trend.

Here are a few things to think about when you come across a diet plan or promise:

* Don't believe the hype. People are often paid to say a diet worked for them, and results for everyone will be different. Always bear in mind that old saying, "If it sounds too good to be true, it probably is."

* Be a critical thinker and arm yourself with a basic understanding of nutrition. If you think something sounds like it wouldn't be good for your body in the long run, trust your instincts!

* Extreme diets aren't usually a good solution if you're trying to achieve a healthy weight. Sensible steps rule—taking good care of your body, eating well, and doing some kind of fun physical activity every day are better strategies for feeling good about yourself, whatever size you are.

WEIGHT MATTERS

It's hard to go very long without hearing about America's obesity epidemic. Undeniably, more Americans and Canadians—adults, teens, and children—are carrying around more weight than ever before: in the U.S., 31 percent of adults, 21 percent of teenagers, and 18 percent of children aged 6-11 are obese. But some nutritionists and public health experts think focusing on obesity is misguided: that it emphasizes how people's bodies *look* rather than how healthy they are. They say that obesity is the result of bad nutrition and not enough exercise, and it's those issues that we should focus on, rather than people's size. The illnesses that often come with obesity, like heart disease and diabetes, are the result of poor eating habits, not of weight alone. There's also evidence that people who don't feel ashamed of their bodies are more likely to improve their health by eating better or exercising.

Campaigns like Strong4Life, based in Atlanta, Georgia, have had great results helping kids and teens to get healthy through better eating and exercise. "Changing my habits wasn't easy," said one participant, Nicholas Weddington, who was diagnosed with borderline diabetes and high blood pressure at 12. "But once I realized bad food actually made me feel bad, it was easier to stay on track."

NEED A CLEANSE? TAKE A SHOWER

WHEN IT COMES TO DIET ADVICE, detoxes and cleanses are the extreme—regimens designed to rid us of the "toxins" and "poisons" that supposedly build up in our bodies. They're popular among some celebrities, and you might have seen ads for them online or in magazines. Cleanses can range from small improvements, like cutting out sugar or caffeine for a few weeks, to very strict fasts, meaning you consume very little food or no food at all. One popular cleanse involves consuming nothing but lemonade spiked with cayenne pepper for 10 days!

Most doctors, however, think cleanses are unnecessary. They point out that we already have a built-in way to eliminate the things our bodies don't need: it's called the digestive system. People using cleanses or fasts as a quick way to lose weight won't get long-lasting results, either. Cleansers do usually drop a few pounds quickly, because their bodies lose water when they aren't eating. You can also lose muscle, and experience unpleasant side effects, like dizziness, headaches, and weakness. People who stay on fasts or restrictive cleanses for a long time, or go on them regularly, can develop serious health problems.

FAST FRIENDS

CAN PEOPLE SURVIVE FOR LONG PERIODS WITHOUT FOOD? Fasting is part of many religious traditions (for example, Muslims fast every day from dawn until sunset during the month of Ramadan) and it's often practiced as a way to develop spiritual discipline. However, the human body usually stops functioning after about three weeks without food, and less time—only about three days—without water. But through the ages, saints, mystics, and others have claimed the ability to go for much longer without eating.

In the late 1800s, there was a strange trend in the U.S. and Britain: a number of preteen and teen women, known as "fasting girls," claimed to be able to survive for months or years with no food, or only tiny amounts. Many also boasted of special powers, like being able to predict the future. (If you didn't eat for a few weeks, you'd probably have strange visions, too.) Several became media celebrities. But when doctors investigated, they caught the girls sneaking small amounts of food, or were otherwise unable to prove that the girls never ate. Today many scholars believe the fasting girls had eating disorders— not so miraculous after all.

In modern times, "breatharians" profess the ability to survive on nothing but sunlight and fresh air, and some practitioners say they can go months without food or even water. But medical tests have never proven anyone can live this way for more than a few days. Experts consider breatharianism a dangerous fraud—several people attempting to follow the "diet" have actually died.

FOOD FOR THOUGHT

Eating a healthy diet is actually pretty simple, but for many people, it seems to be one of the hardest things to do. Most of us know, to some degree, what we should be eating, but actually putting that into practice can be hard, whether because of time or cost, or because fast-food burgers and soft drinks are more appealing than broccoli and water. Let's face it: humans have invented a lot of delicious things to eat that are bad for us, in one way or another. But it might help to know that people who are in the habit of eating well often crave things like veggies, fruit, and whole grains and don't want sweets or greasy snacks as often. And enjoying your food is far more important than counting every gram of fat or sugar. Here are a few ways you can do that:

Focus on being active and eating healthy foods that make you feel good, rather than on your weight.

Don't cut out an entire group of foods, for whatever reason, without talking to a doctor or nutritionist.

Enjoy your food and have fun making it. Try herbs or spices you've never used before, or use colorful fruits and veggies to make your plate into a piece of art. Cookbooks and food websites can provide great inspiration.

CHAPTER 4

FRANKEN-FOOD

SINCE ANCIENT TIMES, people have found ways to make food tastier and keep it edible for longer. In the days before fridges, fermenting, sun-drying, smoking, and preserving with salt were popular techniques. Middle Easterners and Asians sun-dried fruits and vegetables 14,000 years ago, while Plains indigenous tribes in North America hung meat at the top of their teepees, above the fire, to smoke it. None of these people had heard of a molecule or a microorganism, but they were already using the power of chemistry in amazing ways.

Over the past century, we've gotten very good at using science to transform our food, whether it's to make it easier to transport, safer, longer-lasting, tastier, better looking, or more uniform. Today, a lot of our food is created in conditions that resemble a lab more than a kitchen. What does that mean for the way we eat?

SPACE-AGE FOOD

MODERN FOOD PROCESSING owes a lot to the Space Race. In the years after World War II, the U.S. and the former Soviet Union were desperate to outdo each other in the mastery of outer space, and each invested billions in technology that might give them the edge. Astronauts needed food that could stay edible for a long time, and that need led to the development of freeze drying, concentrated juices, and artificial sweeteners, colors, and preservatives.

Want a glimpse of the "can-opener cooking" that became popular back in the day? Dig up a cookbook from the 1950s or '60s (or search the web for vintage recipes) and check out the ingredients—you'll find lots of Jell-O, prepared sauces, and canned soups, fish, and meat.

The first meal in space was eaten by Russian astronaut Yuri Gagarin in 1961. It consisted of three toothpaste-like tubes, two containing puréed meat and one containing chocolate sauce. Yuck! A few years later, American space meals had gotten a bit more gourmet, with astronauts on the Gemini space missions eating freeze-dried, reconstituted shrimp cocktail, chicken, vegetables, and butterscotch pudding.

Back on earth, these innovations led to a boom in "convenience foods." The second half of the 20th century brought frozen TV dinners, a wide variety of canned ready-to-eat foods, and packaged food mixes for things like rice, drinks, and cake—all of which appealed to women who had less time to spend on food preparation, now that they were working outside of the home in greater numbers. These products didn't require complicated cooking knowledge, and promised predictable results: no worrying about whether your cake would rise properly or your soup was too thin.

Before long, processed, neatly packaged food became a status symbol: it showed that you could afford to spend money. Backyard vegetable gardens, and raising chickens—now popular hobbies for foodies—were at the time associated with poor people and immigrants, who grew their own food because they had no other options.

Premade foods have many advantages. Fresh foods like meat and produce spoil quickly and need to be refrigerated, and are more likely to carry microorganisms that can cause illness. Canning, dehydrating, or heat-processing food kills bacteria and microorganisms, and preserved food can be transported long distances and kept unrefrigerated. These techniques also make seasonal fruits and vegetables, like peaches or tomatoes, available all year. But the processing of foods also tends to reduce naturally occurring nutrients; canned fruit, for example, is lower in vitamin C than fresh fruit. Processed foods can also be higher in salt and sugar, and often contain other additives.

THANKS FOR THE MREs

The Space Race is off, but the boundaries of food science are still being pushed—by the military. Meals for troops on duty have a tall order: they need to be lightweight, nutritious, durable enough to be dropped from helicopters, and must stay edible for months or years even in extreme temperatures. So the U.S. Army employs food technologists to come up with food and packaging innovations. Some familiar items were developed this way: M&M's candies were designed especially for U.S. troops in World War II—their hard candy shell kept the chocolate inside from melting in warm temperatures. In the 1990s, they had to be re-engineered to survive the extreme heat of the First Gulf War in Iraq, which was accomplished by reversing the protein and fat in the chocolate molecules.

As for meals, they've come a long way since the days of the American Civil War, when soldiers on long campaigns survived on salted pork and hardtack (a type of cracker sometimes nicknamed "molar breakers"). Today, soldiers eat MREs (Meal, Ready-to-Eat)—dehydrated meals stored in pouches. There are over 20 types, including things like lemon pepper tuna and pesto pasta, with options for vegetarians and religious and cultural preferences. They even come with a flameless heater—a little package of magnesium, salt, and iron that releases heat when water is added.

WITH ADDED INGREDIENTS

ADDITIVES ARE SUBSTANCES ADDED TO PROCESSED FOODS to enhance or preserve their flavor, texture, or appearance. They're part of the reason these foods can be stored for a long time without going rotten. There are around 20 different categories of additives, including natural substances like vitamin C, salt, and vinegar, and others like thickeners, preservatives, and emulsifiers (which prevent mixtures like mayonnaise or ice cream from separating).

To see an example of how additives are used, consider bread. To make bread, you basically need three things: flour, yeast to make it rise, and water. If you want to get fancy, you could add some other grains for texture and variety, and maybe a little salt for flavor. But look at the ingredients list on a package of supermarket bread: chances are it's a lot longer than three or four items, and there might be a few you can't pronounce. Some common ones are azodicarbonamide, a chemical used to improve the texture of bread (and also to give yoga mats their elasticity); L-cysteine, which makes bread softer; potassium bromate, which lessens baking time; monoglycerides and diglycerides, which give a smoother texture and make bread last longer on the shelf; and calcium propionate, which prevents mold growth.

Countless school science projects have proven the results: a slice of additive-laden bread can stay picture-perfect and mold-free for months, while a home-baked loaf turns green and fuzzy or dries out in under a week.

The safety of food additives has been debated for years. For instance, boric acid was a common preservative in the 1800s and early 1900s—until people realized it was toxic. And the food dye Red No. 2 was banned in the U.S. in the 1970s after it was found to cause cancer in rats at high doses. Both the Food and Drug Administration in the U.S. and Health Canada ban additives that cause cancer in humans or animals, but sometimes the data isn't clear right away. And some additives are legal even though they've been linked to health risks: sodium nitrite, for instance, which is added to processed meats like salami and sausages to give them their reddish pink color, has been shown to increase the risk of cancer and heart disease in humans.

Food dyes are one area of controversy. Synthetic, or artificial, dyes are usually more effective and cheaper than colors made from natural sources, but there is disagreement about which are safe to use. Some have been linked to allergic reactions, and one study found that a synthetic yellow color called tartrazine made children hyperactive. Norway and Sweden ban food dyes completely; the United Kingdom, the U.S., and Canada all permit different ones.

As for preservatives, you could argue that whatever risks come from consuming a small amount are outweighed by the benefits of food lasting longer, and fewer people becoming sick from eating spoiled food. However, there are many canned, dried, and packaged foods that don't contain preservatives, so it's possible to avoid them if you read labels carefully.

Milk is white—so why is most cheddar cheese orange? Back in the old days, cows fed on pasture produced yellowish milk in the spring and summer because of beta carotene (a vitamin) in fresh grass. In the winter, the cows were fed on hay, and their milk was paler. The yellower cheese produced from spring milk was seen as better, so in the 1800s dairy farmers started adding color to their cheese (first in the form of annatto seeds, and later as synthetic color) to make it more appealing to buyers. Competing cheddar makers kept trying to out-dye each other until the cheese ended up the familiar pumpkin hue we know today.

PASTEURIZATION

One important way of preserving food was developed in 1864 by the French chemist Louis Pasteur. Pasteurization involves heating liquids (like milk or juice) for a short time, then cooling them. The heat kills most microorganisms and helps prevent the growth of harmful bacteria like salmonella and E. coli, which would normally thrive in the liquid, and which can cause severe food poisoning. Before pasteurization, every year thousands of children and adults became sick or died from drinking raw milk. Some people claim that raw, unprocessed milk has more health benefits, as the pasteurization process destroys some of milk's vitamins, minerals, and helpful bacteria. But unpasteurized milk is considered among the most risky foods for contracting food-borne illnesses, and its sale is banned in Canada and many states in the U.S.

FLAVOR WIZARDS

Ever wonder about those "natural and artificial flavors" you see on ingredient lists for yogurt, fruit drinks, candy, and snacks? They're the creations of flavorists, food scientists who work in laboratories creating the chemical compounds that trick our taste buds into thinking we're tasting strawberry when we're chewing a piece of gum, or guacamole on tortilla chips. Flavorings are often used to make food with lower fat, sugar, or salt content more appealing to consumers, and they're a huge part of the snack industry, which is constantly pushing to come up with new and unique flavors. Food flavoring labs sell specific flavors—the formulas for which are kept highly secret—for huge sums to food manufacturers like Coca-Cola, Gatorade, and General Mills. Flavorists are also working on experimental new foods, like gum that would change flavor three times while it's chewed.

FAT, SUGAR, SALT

ALMOST ALL PROCESSED FOOD in our supermarkets contains certain amounts of fat (usually some type of vegetable oil), sugar or other sweetener, and salt. In the right proportions, these three ingredients have the power to make food almost irresistible.

Why? Turns out we're designed to seek out fat and sugar, which are high in calories, and which we wouldn't have found that often back in our plant-foraging days. When we taste these foods, all the programming of our evolution tells us: "Eat more!" Today, however, sugar and fat aren't exactly in short supply, so our hardwired attraction to them backfires. Our bodies tell us to eat more, but eating too much can make us sick.

Manufacturers of everything from fast-food hamburgers to breakfast cereal and chips have spent huge amounts of money researching the exact amounts and proportions of these ingredients that will hit our taste buds and brain in just the right way—in the food industry they call this the "bliss point"—and make us want to eat more.

So next time you open a bag of chips and can't stop at one, you know why!

When companies offer "healthier" products with less of one of these ingredients, they'll often increase the proportion of another to make up for it in the taste department. For instance, low-fat yogurt often has more sugar, and low-salt products can still have a lot of fat and sugar. Food company executives can't win, in a way: they're criticized for hooking people on junk food, but they know nobody will buy those foods if they don't taste good, and their iconic snacks, drinks, and cereals simply wouldn't taste the same without good doses of unhealthy ingredients. The good news is that a few companies, like Kraft, have had some success in modifying their recipes to cut back on sugar, fat, and salt.

Meanwhile, scientists at big companies like Nestlé and Cargill are trying to find ever more ways to make their products irresistible. Their experiments include engineering fat globules to improve how food feels in the mouth, and tinkering with salt and sugar molecules so they deliver a faster hit to the taste buds. Frito-Lay has even hired a neuromarketing firm—which uses brain-scanning technology to analyze how people react to their snack foods, and pinpoint how things like color and texture light up the pleasure centers of our brains.

Some snack and drink companies like to get their customers involved in the quest for new taste sensations. Every year Lay's lets budding flavor wizards submit ideas for new potato chip flavors, and people vote online for their favorites. The winner gets $50,000 and their chip flavor manufactured by Lay's. The flavor finalists for 2014 included Bacon Poutine and Cinnamon Bun.

INFOBITES
PROCESSED VS. FRESH

PERCENTAGE OF AMERICANS' SUPERMARKET DOLLARS SPENT ON PROCESSED FOOD

 **90%**

AMERICANS' FOOD CONSUMPTION, BY CALORIES:

12.5%
fruits, vegetables, grains, beans, nuts, seeds

25.5%
meat, fish, dairy, eggs

62%
processed food

ADDITIVES

APPROXIMATE NUMBER OF FOOD ADDITIVES APPROVED FOR USE:

U.S.: 3,000

Canada: 850
European Union: 350

GM FOODS

MOST COMMONLY GENETICALLY MODIFIED FOODS:

Corn   Soy   Zucchini   Alfalfa   Canola   Sugar beets   Milk

ARTIFICIALLY SWEET

N 1952, **THE KIRSCH BOTTLING COMPANY** in Brooklyn, New York, launched a product the likes of which no one had ever seen—a sugar-free ginger ale named No-Cal. Other companies quickly got in on the act, and soon, soda drinkers could guzzle Diet Rite, diet Dr Pepper, Tab, Fresca, and others, all without worrying about that extra sugar (and what it was doing to their waistlines). Since then, food companies have spent countless dollars developing products that promise to let us eat the kinds of food we tend to crave, like sugary and fatty treats, without the side effect of calories.

Artificial sweeteners like sucralose and aspartame are at least as sweet as sugar but contain virtually no calories—the molecules pass through the body without being digested—and aren't harmful to teeth. They're commonly found in diet soft drinks and gum, and in convenient one-serving packages we can stir into coffee or tea.

While there are lots of unproven health warnings and rumors about the dangers of unnatural sweeteners, aspartame and sucralose have been repeatedly tested and are generally considered safe in the quantities people normally eat them. Whether they actually keep people from gaining weight, however, is up for debate. Some scientists believe artificial sweeteners mess with our metabolisms, because their sweet taste triggers the promise of calories they never deliver. But more research is needed to figure out how this happens.

FAKE FATS

In the 1990s, there was a craze for low-fat food, and food manufacturers responded by filling grocery shelves with low-fat products. They also developed a product called Olestra, a fat that can't be metabolized (it passes straight through your body, without delivering calories). Olestra started turning up in high-fat foods like chips and crackers, with the promise that snack lovers could finally eat as much of these foods as they wanted without guilt. Unfortunately, the side effects of consuming Olestra included abdominal cramping and diarrhea, which, understandably, made the ingredient a bit unpopular. But you can still find Olestra (sometimes under the brand name Olean) in a few potato chip and snack products on grocery shelves. Just make sure you're near a bathroom if you decide to give it a try!

A FUTURE WITHOUT FOOD?

I N **THE JETSONS,** a 1960s animated TV series about a family living in a high-tech future, science has finally solved the inconvenient problem of having to eat regularly to survive; the cartoon characters simply pop a pill containing all their nutrient needs. No cooking, no mess! More ominously, in the old sci-fi film *Soylent Green*, people in a futuristic society survive on green wafers produced by a scary, controlling corporation. (SPOILER ALERT! It turns out the wafers are made from people!)

Back in the real world, it's not so easy to fit our complex nutritional needs into a capsule—you'd have to swallow at least half a pound of pills a day to get enough calories to survive, which seems a lot more inconvenient than simply eating a sandwich. But the idea of food replacements has been around for a while: the powdered, vitamin-enhanced orange drink Tang, for instance, was developed in the 1950s to provide astronauts with nutrients in space. Today, meal replacement drinks and bars are common among dieters, athletes, and people rushing out the door with no time for breakfast.

Recently, a California entrepreneur raised over $1 million to produce a nutrient-packed shake that he claims can almost entirely replace solid food. (In a nod to the old sci-fi film, the drink is called Soylent, though the nutrition label says it "contains no people.") The advertised advantages of replacing most of your food with Soylent? It's cheaper than groceries, convenient, and environmentally friendly, and can also help you lose weight. It's also been promoted as a way to help people around the world dealing with food shortages or famines. Many nutritionists, however, say that the way real food nourishes our bodies is much too complex to be replicated by a nutrient cocktail. And while a vitamin shake might fill up your stomach, you probably won't be tossing out the pizza menus and hosting Friday-night Soylent parties anytime soon.

ALTERED GENES

THE MOST DRAMATIC CHANGES we've made to our food have been introduced in the last two decades. People have been modifying crops for a long time—from the earliest farming of certain grains to the development of hybrid fruits and vegetables. Genetic modification of food is different, however; it modifies plants and animals by changing the structure of their DNA, the basic building blocks for every living thing. Genetic modification can make produce easier to transport, improve nutrition and yield, and make crops more resistant to viruses, pests, and herbicides. Currently, soy, corn, and canola—a grain grown for the oil in its seeds—have been genetically modified more than any other foods. A number of fruits and vegetables have also been modified, including tomatoes, zucchini, and papaya, which was altered to resist a virus that threatened to wipe out Hawaii's papaya industry.

Strong opinions and fears about genetically modified (GM) foods are widespread. Between the corporate hype of GM producers and the alarming claims made by GM opponents, it can be difficult to figure out what's true. Some environmental organizations and consumer groups worry that the long-term risks of genetically modified foods aren't known.

They also express concern about giant multinational corporations owning the rights to GM seeds and controlling the food supply.

Most scientists agree that GM food isn't any less safe to eat than conventional food, and that GM technology is essential for increasing crop production to meet the demands of a growing population, especially in the developing world. They say GM crops will benefit society by permitting less use of pesticides and water, and improving food security. GM opponents, however, say that there's no proof genetic modification will actually achieve these things. Some also argue that GM foods are part of the Big Food approach to farming that promotes fewer varieties of crops and less biodiversity. A more sustainable food system, they say, would work *with* the environment rather than attempting to control it.

Hybrid varieties of fruits or vegetables are made by cross-pollinating one plant to another. A few you might have come across at the grocery store: pluots (a plum-apricot cross), tangelos (a hybrid of tangerine and pomelo grapefruit), and broccoflower (broccoli crossed with cauliflower).

BEEF FROM A LAB?

Could your burger one day come from a lab instead of a live animal? Scientists are working on it, but the result probably won't show up in supermarkets for at least a decade or two. Lab-grown meat is produced by taking cells from animal muscle, then dosing them with a mixture of blood and antibiotics to make the cells replicate and grow. Doesn't sound too appetizing, but the benefits are promising: cultured meat may one day produce the same amount as farmed meat using a fraction of the land, water, and energy. Taste tests have gotten a thumbs-down so far, but with support from the co-founder of Google, animal rights organizations, and even NASA, investors think it's only a matter of time before the dream of a petri-dish steak becomes a reality.

In the meantime, there are many meat substitutes made from plant ingredients, like grains, soy, and pea protein. They can be found in most grocery stores, and as of 2013, more than a third of people in the U.S. reported eating them, either as a substitute for or alongside real meat.

FOOD FOR THOUGHT

Science can do amazing things. Breakthroughs in knowledge and technology have made the food we eat much more convenient, sanitary, and tasty. Think of all the foods you eat in a day that are the product of technology: cereal in a box, pasteurized milk or juice, chips, ketchup, boxed pasta, frozen pizza, ice cream ... imagine the time and effort it would take if you had to make all those things from scratch! The ultra-convenience certainly makes our lives easy, but here are some things to keep in mind as you look for a healthy balance.

A good way to eat fewer additives and less salt, sugar, and unhealthy fats is to eat less processed food overall. For snacks, trade chips or cookies from a package for a piece of fruit, vegetables, or plain nuts.

Try to get in the habit of reading labels, and look up ingredients you don't recognize. Not all hard-to-pronounce ingredients are unnatural or harmful, but it's good to know what you're eating and why it's in your food.

You can try your own experiment to show the effect of additives like tartrazine (page 112). You'll need three friends and a watch or timer. Have your friends measure their pulse (at wrist or neck): how many times does their heart beat in one minute? Write it down. Have one friend drink a cup of orange pop, one eat some Doritos, and one eat a cookie or piece of fruit. Wait 10 minutes, then have them take their pulses again. Did any of the foods have more of an effect than the others?

CHAPTER 5

THE SECRETS OF SELLING

FOR A LONG TIME, PEOPLE IN THE FOOD BUSINESS shared a common concern. Our stomachs, they knew, were only so big, which meant there was a limit to how much food they could sell us. With clever marketing, you could convince people that they needed to own more shoes, or even a second car. But you couldn't make people buy more food than their bodies could physically handle, so there was only so much profit the food business could make. Right?

Well, not exactly. It turns out you *can* convince people to buy more food than they need, and the food industry has gotten very good at doing just that. Massive amounts of money are spent persuading us to buy as much as possible, while a great deal of time and effort goes into researching exactly the right way to appeal to consumers: what packaging to use, what flavors and colors, what kind of advertising, and how and where to target them. A good portion of that effort—about $1.8 billion a year in the U.S.—is aimed at kids and teenagers, and it tends to promote the kind of sugary, refined, high-fat food that adults often tell you *not* to eat. Talk about mixed messages!

Food marketers used to reach kids through TV, where they had to follow all kinds of rules about what they could promote and say. Now, however, they've got the Internet, which lets them connect with you pretty much anywhere, and anytime. They can even use what they learn through your online activities to fine-tune their message, targeting you in exactly the way they think will make you pull out your wallet. But how, and why, do they do this?

Marketers who try to entice shoppers with cool new food and drink concepts don't always come up with winners. Just a few of the failed products that have gone down history's garbage disposal: colored ketchup in shades of green, blue, and purple; baby-food-style jars for adults with individual servings of beef burgundy and vegetables; breakfast cola; toaster bacon; and celery-flavored Jell-O.

BROUGHT TO YOU BY...

Beef. It's What's for Dinner."
"*Pork. The Other White Meat.*"
"*Milk: It Does a Body Good.*"

Sound familiar? Food advertisements—like many others—have a way of getting stuck in your head. Think about some of the memorable ones you've seen: an ad for a packaged food or drink, like Doritos or Dr Pepper, or maybe a restaurant, like Taco Bell. You might also remember the slogan for a particular type of food (like the ones above), or the long-running "Got Milk?" campaign, which featured all sorts of celebrities sporting milk moustaches. In fact, marketing campaigns can have a huge effect on how we eat and think about our food.

In North America, farmers who produce a certain type of food, like beef or potatoes, often band together to form marketing boards and industry groups—for instance, the National Chicken Council in the U.S., or the Dairy Farmers of Ontario. These groups often try to get laws passed that help their industry, and they spend a lot of money marketing to shoppers. They might buy ad space on TV or in magazines, put out cookbooks or recipes, or persuade journalists to do features or news stories, all to get people to see their product in a positive light and eat more of it.

Sometimes their efforts are aimed at "rebranding" a food, or convincing consumers to see it in a different way. The pork slogan above was used in ad campaigns for the National Pork Board starting in the late 1980s. At the time, many people thought of "white" meat, like chicken or turkey, as healthier and lighter than "red" meat, like beef. The U.S. Department of Agriculture (USDA), along with most nutritionists, classifies pork as a red meat, since it comes from a mammal. But the National Pork Board took advantage of the fact that pork often turns a lighter color when it's cooked to come up with a slogan that would make people start thinking of it as a healthy, lean "white" meat. It seemed to work; in the 12 years after the ads started running, Americans' pork consumption went up by 20 percent, while their beef consumption went down.

Rebranding can also mean changing a food's name. Prunes, for instance, long associated with old ladies and constipation remedies, have recently been reinvented on food packages as the more appealing "dried plums." Or sometimes it's a matter of convincing people to use an ingredient in different ways.

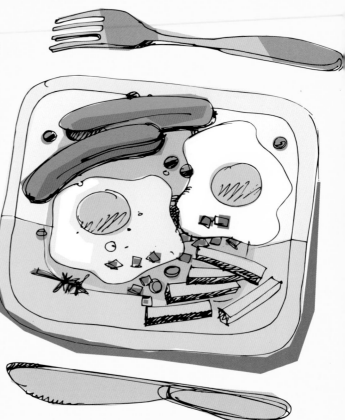

For example, the American Egg Board was concerned that people were eating eggs only on weekends, so they created an ad campaign aimed at getting parents to cook eggs for their kids on weekday mornings, too. Other campaigns have encouraged people to eat eggs for dinner.

Sometimes producers try to boost a food's health image. Chocolate milk, for instance, contains a lot of added sugar, and is usually considered just a sweet treat for kids. But a 2014 ad campaign by the Dairy Farmers of Canada called "Recharge with Milk" portrays chocolate milk as a kind of energy drink, suitable for athletes refueling after a strenuous marathon or weight-training session.

Restaurants sometimes rebrand themselves, too. The fast-food chain formerly known as Kentucky Fried Chicken changed its name to KFC in 1991, partly to downplay the greasy images conjured up by the word "fried" at a time when fatty food was getting a lot of bad press. Now, how about a nice bucket of F'd C?

RAISIN ATTENTION

Would you believe that when your parents were growing up, some of the biggest celebrities around were a group of singing, dancing raisins invented as a way to sell more dried fruit? Yes, it's true (it was a strange time). In the 1980s, raisin growers in California came up with an ad campaign designed to ditch the wrinkly raisin's boring and uncool image. They introduced the California Raisins—dancing claymation characters who sang classic Motown songs like "I Heard It Through the Grapevine." For a while, the Raisins were bigger than Mickey Mouse, spawning stuffed toys, figurines, lunchboxes, clothing, posters, bedsheets, a comic-book series, two award-winning TV specials, and several top-selling albums. Pretty good for a bunch of shriveled grapes!

The California Raisins starred in several TV specials, including this one from 1989.

BRAND NEW BRANDS

MOST OF THE FOOD ADVERTISING we see isn't for ingredients like milk or beef, but for food brands. And that kind of advertising is actually pretty new: it all got started with the self-serve grocery stores we talked about back in chapter 1. Once consumers started picking their own products off store shelves rather than having them scooped into plain bags from a bulk bin by a store clerk, "branding" became an important way for shoppers to tell one product from another. The first way food companies did this was by using logos, often with a person on them—think of Quaker Oats, Aunt Jemima, Uncle Ben, or Betty Crocker, all of which originally had a person's face on the package that customers would recognize and trust.

At the time, food advertising tended to focus on the product's claimed benefits. Print ads in magazines and newspapers often had paragraphs of text describing why the brand was trustworthy, and superior to its competitors. Since then, food advertising has become much more visual: an ad on TV or on a billboard might not tell you anything about the food at all, instead relying on a mouthwatering picture of a burger or an ice cream sundae. Food marketers know that the best way to your wallet is through your stomach.

A Quaker Oats trade card—a small card companies would give to potential customers—from 1895.

Marketing these days also focuses a lot more on what's called "brand identification": trying to appeal to the way we see ourselves—or want to see ourselves—so we identify with the product. An energy drink ad might show someone playing sports, with pulse-pounding music. An ad for cereal promoted as healthy might feature a slim woman doing yoga or wrapping a measuring tape around her waist. An ad for a pizza restaurant might focus on a group of teenagers laughing and having fun. In each case, the ad is promoting not so much the food as a lifestyle it's meant to represent: buy this product, they say, and your life will be like this.

READY FOR ITS CLOSE-UP

As delicious as the burgers in fast-food ads look, you wouldn't want to eat them! Those picture-perfect sandwiches are primped and fussed over for hours by professional "food stylists" before the ad is shot. If you actually bit into one you'd get a mouthful of nearly raw meat (so the burger stays plump), cardboard (to keep the bun from getting soggy), pins and glue (to keep lettuce and sesame seeds in place), and dye (for a tempting color).

YOGURT FOR EVERYONE

YOGURT IS A GREAT EXAMPLE of how brand identification works. Let's review the basics: yogurt is made from cultured milk. It's nutritious and tasty and most people like it. Some people might prefer plain or strawberry or vanilla, but they're all basically the same product. So yogurt companies should advertise to almost everyone, right?

Instead, the yogurt aisle at the supermarket shows how specific food marketing can be. There's pricey organic yogurt aimed at environmentally and health-conscious people, and non-dairy yogurt for vegans or people with food sensitivities. There's low-fat yogurt for dieters and Greek yogurt for trend followers. There's flavored yogurt in a tube for kids, as well as drinkable yogurt in dinosaur-shaped bottles. There's a brand of yogurt marketed to women, which makes the unusual promise that it helps you have regular bowel movements (seriously). And there's yogurt in macho-looking black packages marketed specifically to men—who presumably wouldn't be caught dead buying the yogurt that helps women's digestion.

Try to find a container of plain, regular yogurt—it's not as easy as you might think!

So why is there a different brand of yogurt for practically every group imaginable? Well, in a market where lots of companies are producing the same thing, it can be an advantage to have a smaller piece of that market. Rather than appealing to everyone, these brands focus on a very specific group of people, and create packaging, advertising imagery, and marketing to speak to them (and only them).

The old expression "sex sells" apparently applies to food, too. Restaurants including Carl's Jr., Burger King, and Pizza Hut have tried to grab the attention of young men by using bikini-clad women and seriously suggestive images in their ads. Though it's most often female bodies on show, Kraft did some equal-opportunity exploiting with a controversial salad dressing ad that featured a ripped naked man, covered only by the strategically placed corner of a picnic blanket.

DECODING THE PACKAGE

Made With FREE RANGE CHICKEN

TODAY, MORE PEOPLE THAN EVER want to eat healthy food, and are concerned about things like pesticides, preservatives, fats, and sugars. Many people also want to eat responsibly, avoiding meat or eggs produced in cramped conditions, for instance, or seafood that was fished in a way that harms other aquatic animals. Food companies know this, which is why a lot of advertising and packaging now uses words and images that suggest the product is healthy or good for the planet.

The U.S. Department of Agriculture, the Food and Drug Administration, and the Canadian Food Inspection Agency all regulate what food manufacturers can say in their advertising and on packaging. Their claims have to be true, and shouldn't use misleading words or images. But food advertisers (all advertisers, really) know how to follow the rules, and how to work around them. Here are some terms and techniques you might see and what you should know about them.

✳ **LIGHT:** "Light" or "lite" versions of products usually have fewer calories or less fat than the regular version. For canned fruit, these words can mean less sugar. But products can also be described as "light-tasting," which has nothing to do with how nutritious they are.

✳ **LOWER IN, LESS THAN:** Food marketers often use comparisons when advertising lower-fat, lower-sodium, or lower-sugar versions of their regular products. But just because the amount is "lower" doesn't mean it's "low"; low-sugar jam, for example, usually still contains a lot of sugar. Check the nutrition label to figure out how much salt, sugar, or fat is really in a serving.

* **NATURE, NATURAL:** These terms are often used to suggest nutritional superiority to health-conscious consumers, although "natural" doesn't always mean healthy. According to Canadian regulations, food described as natural shouldn't contain artificial flavors or additives, or synthetic vitamins and minerals. But "natural" foods can be high in sugar, sodium, and saturated fat. In the U.S., "natural" has no defined meaning for food advertising, so it doesn't tell you anything about a product.

* **MADE WITH WHOLE GRAIN:** Usually means the product isn't made completely with whole grains; otherwise it would likely be labeled as "100% whole grain." Same goes for "made with real fruit": fruit or juice may be an ingredient in a candy or cereal bar, but it's not necessarily a primary ingredient. Check the label: if white flour (often called enriched flour) appears first on the list of ingredients, you'll know the product isn't mostly whole-grain.

* **NO TRANS FAT, CHOLESTEROL FREE:** Products free of these substances can still be high in saturated fat. Cholesterol is found only in foods that come from animals, so crackers fried in vegetable oil and cookies made with palm oil will be cholesterol free, even though they're likely high in fat.

FREE RANGE, CAGE FREE: Chickens raised for meat need access to the outdoors to be certified as free range, but for egg-laying chickens, there's no common standard. "Cage free," meanwhile, may simply mean the birds were raised in high densities on a factory floor rather than being stacked in cages. If you want more information on how a company's hens were raised, contact the company online.

 DOLPHIN SAFE: Many cans of tuna feature this label, but there's no independent group keeping an eye on the situation. Also, the labels don't say anything about animals other than dolphins that might be caught in tuna nets, or about whether the fish was caught in an environmentally friendly way. Some groups are working toward clarifying tuna labels: the National Oceanic and Atmospheric Administration in the U.S. has even started a tracking program involving high-school students to make sure dolphin-safe claims on tuna cans are true.

 ORGANIC: To claim "organic" status, products have to be certified according to standards set by either the USDA or the Canadian Food Inspection Agency. A food has to contain at least 95 percent organic ingredients to be able to say it's organic on the label. If the percentage is between 70 and 95 percent, manufacturers can claim it "contains organic ingredients." Again, be aware that "organic" doesn't always mean healthy—organic cereal can be high in sugar, for instance, and organic potato chips usually have as much fat and salt as regular versions.

✳ **PURE:** If a product says "pure corn oil" or "100% pure," it has to be 100 percent made of that ingredient. If it says "made with pure corn oil," however, it means pure corn oil was used along with a preservative or other ingredients.

✳ **SUGAR SPLITTING:** Ingredients are listed on a food label by quantity—in other words, by how much of the ingredient is in the product. But many processed foods contain several different forms of sugars: high-fructose corn syrup, invert sugar, and dextrose, for instance. If you lumped all of those together under one heading, "sugar" might be the first ingredient listed; split them, though, and they appear lower on the list. Checking the total amount of added sugar on the label will give you a clearer picture.

None of these terms mean a product is bad, of course, or that advertisers are lying to you. But it's good to be aware of how advertising works. Next time you notice certain words drawing you in, look at the language critically and read ingredients lists and nutrition boxes carefully. Does it change the way you look at the food?

INFOBITES
ADS EVERYWHERE

Average number of food ads U.S. teens see per week:

 **112**

Average number of those ads that are for fruits and vegetables:

1

TOP FOOD PRODUCT CATEGORIES ADVERTISED TO YOUNG PEOPLE

High-sugar breakfast cereals   Fast-food restaurants

Candy   Sugary drinks

RANK OF FOOD COMPANIES AMONG TOP 25 U.S. ADVERTISERS, BY SPENDING (2012)

#4 McDonald's ($957 million)   #19 Subway ($516 million)

ADVERTISING DOLLARS

Amount spent to advertise fast food (U.S., 2012):

4.6 BILLION

Amount spent to advertise fruits and vegetables:

116 MILLION

FAST-FOOD CONSUMPTION

41% of teens eat fast food every day

HAVE SOME SODA FRUIT

One ad campaign for 7UP stretched the limits of the word "natural" to the breaking point. The soft drink was promoted as "all natural," and the image in the ad showed a can of the stuff growing on a tree along with fruit. The drink's primary ingredient, however, is high-fructose corn syrup. High-fructose corn syrup may be derived from corn, which is natural, but the ingredient goes through a complex industrial process before being added to food; implying it's as natural as fruit growing on a tree is highly misleading. Following controversy about the claim and the threat of a lawsuit from the Center for Science in the Public Interest, the company changed its message, and now says only that 7UP has "100% natural flavors."

SUPERFOODS TO THE RESCUE

CHANCES ARE YOU'VE HEARD THE WORD "SUPERFOOD" applied to things like blueberries, kale, or dark chocolate. It's used to describe foods that supposedly have terrific health benefits, and that are sometimes even said to cure medical conditions or prevent diseases. If you pay attention to food trends, you'll start to see a pattern: a study comes out showing that eating goji berries, for instance, or drinking green tea, might have a good effect on your health. There are lots of news stories about it. Then the superfood starts to pop up in all sorts of food products: goji berry yogurt and granola bars, cookies made with green tea extract, and so on, all claiming to have the benefits proved in the study. Pretty soon the superfood is everywhere.

In truth, the term "superfood" is a brilliant marketing tool. It's not that these foods aren't good for you. Berries, for example, are high in vitamin C, and kale is a great source of minerals and vitamins. It's simply that no food can possibly do everything that superfood promoters claim, and many of the benefits attached to them—like preventing or curing cancer—are scientifically unproven. Superfoods can also unbalance your diet if you eat too much of them, and certain ones could even be harmful if eaten in large amounts.

OUT OF JUICE

When is pomegranate juice not pomegranate juice? The U.S. Supreme Court had to answer that bizarre question in a 2014 false advertising case against Coca-Cola. The product at issue was a drink that claimed to be a "Pomegranate Blueberry Flavored Blend of Five Juices." The label on the bottle features pictures of these fruits, and the words "Pomegranate Blueberry" are much larger than the rest. But the actual amount of pomegranate and blueberry juice in the bottle? Barely enough to fill an eyedropper.

The competitor suing Coca-Cola said this was misleading to consumers, and that the company was trying to take advantage of the healthy reputation of pomegranate and blueberry juices while using mostly cheaper ingredients. Coca-Cola argued that since the drink was pomegranate and blueberry "flavored," there was nothing wrong with their labeling. But the Supreme Court sided with the competitor; all nine judges agreed that Coca-Cola could be sued for false advertising.

THINK FAST!

A BIG PORTION OF THE FOOD ADVERTISING WE SEE is for fast-food restaurant chains like McDonald's, Taco Bell, Subway, and Pizza Hut. While many of these restaurants now offer healthier menu options, like fruit smoothies and salads, the bulk of their menus—and the foods most often featured in their advertising—are high in calories, saturated fat, salt, and sugar.

McDonald's, Wendy's, and Subway all advertise during kids' TV shows and try to reach young children with branded online "advergames" and mobile apps. McDonald's spends more money advertising to kids than to adults or teens; on average, children between 6 and 11 saw more than 300 TV ads for McDonald's in 2012, and preschoolers saw around 260. Fast-food advertising also seeks out teens on social media: in 2012, 6 billion fast-food ads appeared on Facebook, and 3 fast-food chains—Starbucks, McDonald's, and Subway—are in the top 12 of all "liked" brands. They also have millions of followers on Twitter and YouTube—Taco Bell alone has 14 million YouTube views for its ads.

Fast-food chains are increasingly singling out specific groups of young people who they think are especially likely to be good customers. Often that means kids and teens from lower-income families, who might be drawn to eat fast food more often because it's cheap. The companies find out everything about these kids: how they dress, what kind of music they listen to, the TV programs they watch, the slang they use—and then they create ad campaigns featuring people who look like them, doing the things they like to do.

These days, African-American and Hispanic kids and teens are the groups most likely to be bombarded by fast-food ads. And it's likely no coincidence that these groups are considered to be at high risk for diet-related health problems. Companies like KFC and Burger King place lots of ads during Spanish-language kids' programs, and have cut their advertising on English channels. Some companies also run more ads during TV programs popular with black youth; in 2012, African-American kids and teens saw an estimated 60 percent more fast-food ads than white kids.

Food companies—both big and small—often sponsor sports events, concerts, or festivals, usually donating money or products in exchange for free advertising. For the companies, it can be a way to get people to associate their brand with an activity they enjoy. However, some people have criticized fast-food sponsorship of events like the Olympic Games and the World Cup, saying it promotes unhealthy eating at events where the focus should be on athleticism.

FAST-FOOD MAKEOVER

For years, fast-food chains have known that bright red and yellow colors, bright lighting, and noise tend to make people eat more food—and to eat it quickly, making way for more customers. In a 2012 study, part of a fast-food restaurant was transformed with dimmer lighting and soft jazz music. People spent more time eating, but ate less food overall, and rated the experience as more enjoyable than people in the regular, brightly lit area of the restaurant did. Clearly, *where* you eat can have a big effect on *how* you eat—something owners of restaurants, from burger chains to gourmet bistros, have to consider.

ME AND MY BRAND

BRAND IDENTIFICATION IS A BIG PART of how marketing works on social media. By asking you to like or follow their product or restaurant chain on Instagram, Facebook, Twitter, or YouTube, food companies are really asking you to claim their brand as part of your identity—no different from the music you like or activities you do. They entice you by offering coupons, discounts, or contests, and you might enjoy keeping up on when your favorite restaurant is opening a new location, or a brand of soft drink you like tests a new flavor. In return, these companies get some of the same privileges as your friends. Depending on your online privacy settings, they can access your contact lists, mine your conversations with friends for information, and collect data on your online behavior. Then they use that information to understand what teens like and respond to, so they can keep you as a customer and sell more products.

Because technology and teen culture keep changing, food manufacturers have to stay ahead of the curve to keep reaching you with their messages. Here are some examples of strategies they use.

 THEY CREATE ONLINE ENVIRONMENTS. McDonald's, for instance, had a tie-in promotional campaign with the film *Avatar* that included an interactive site where people could play  virtual reality games using a webcam. By buying Big Macs and Happy Meals, they got codes that unlocked special features on the website. The campaign was a success; sales of Big Macs in the U.S. went up by 18 percent.

❋ **THEY WANT YOU TO SHARE.** Mountain Dew launched a viral marketing campaign across social media sites called "DEWmocracy." Kids who signed up were asked to tell their friends and followers on social media to vote on the look and taste of a new drink. Later the company created a private social network for super-fans who "eat, drink, sleep Mountain Dew," according to a company executive. The aim was to use these teens as volunteer salespeople who would promote Mountain Dew to their friends and social networks.

* **THEY TRACK YOUR DATA AND BEHAVIOR ONLINE.** Websites use files called cookies to keep track of things like what sites you visit and how long you stay. They don't know personal details like your name, but they can tell when you visit again from the same phone or computer, and show you advertising they think you'll respond to. And if you sign up for any kind of contest or rewards program online, say for a restaurant or food brand, you'll probably have to provide personal information, like your email address and age. This gives the company data that they can use to tailor ads specifically to you. "We're especially targeting a teen or young adult audience," said a Coca-Cola executive about their online rewards program. "They're always on their mobile phones and they spend an inordinate amount of time on the Internet."

* THEY REACH YOU THROUGH YOUR PHONE. Cell phones have the advantage (to advertisers, and maybe your parents) of being with you all the time. If you give a company access to your details on social media, they can use mobile locating technology to see when you're near one of their restaurants and send you messages with discounts and free items. They can also send you messages at times of day when you're likely to be hungry and more open to suggestion. Coke even has a program to target consumers in locations based on temperature—when it's hot, people might be especially tempted by the idea of a refreshing drink. Restaurant chains also encourage you to "check in" at a restaurant on social media by giving rewards and loyalty points. In return, they get a mention that goes to all your friends and followers, giving them free advertising with your name on it.

* THEY REACH INTO YOUR SUBCONSCIOUS. A lot of advertising research is focused on "neuromarketing," which aims to get around your rational mind and trigger impulses to buy. Marketing researchers use brain activity scans and facial analysis to detect people's responses to ads and fine-tune their message. Weird, but true.

Product placement is a stealth way for food companies to get your attention. Whenever you see Coke cups on the judges' table in a TV talent show, watch characters walk out of a restaurant in a movie, or see a billboard in the background of a video game, chances are the advertiser has paid for the privilege. Kids and teens see hundreds of product placements for junk food on TV every year, two-thirds of them for soft drinks alone.

The case of the disappearing strawberry? One study found that half of foods and drinks marketed to kids with images of fruit on their packages actually contained no fruit ingredients at all. Another fifth of the foods contained only a minimal amount of fruit.

EAT YOUR VEGGIES!

Not all food marketing aimed at kids is for unhealthy treats. There are various programs to promote eating fruits and vegetables, including an online contest that challenged kids to come up with original vegetable recipes. Another asked kids to pledge on social media sites to eat at least one vegetable a day for a month (still a low goal, since food guides recommend at least five servings of fruits and vegetables daily). Studies show that people who see ads encouraging them to eat more fruits and veggies are more likely to meet their five-a-day minimum than people who haven't.

AT THE STORE

NEXT TIME YOU WALK THROUGH A GROCERY STORE, keep track of which products grab your attention first. At the ends of aisles, you'll most likely see displays with discounted bags of chips, or two-for-one bottles of soda. In the cereal aisle, the colorful boxes at your eye level will be well-known brands spiked with sugar, while healthier or no-name options, like oatmeal or puffed rice, may hide near your feet. And while waiting in line to check out, you'll be standing right next to racks of magazines, chocolate bars, candy, and gum.

None of this is an accident. Supermarkets have lots of strategies to get shoppers to buy more than what they had on their grocery list, and to steer them toward more expensive prepared foods instead of things like plain rice, or vegetables. Whole fields of marketing study have sprung up around how to arrange a supermarket's layout to grab customers' attention and get them to buy as much as possible. Factors include where to put the most popular products so people don't cause traffic jams around them, how to stack or arrange the products, which products to put next to each other, and what colors to use in signs and lighting. And those products that grab your attention first? Food manufacturers have probably paid the grocery store to have them placed at eye level, or at the ends of aisles where people can't miss them.

Discounts, coupons, and two-for-one sales are other ways stores encourage people to buy more. It's human nature to want to take advantage of a good offer. Sale prices can be a win-win for the shopper and the store; shopping a sale is a great way to stock up on a staple that keeps well and you use regularly, like dried pasta or canned beans, or items you can freeze, like berries or meat. But if a sale convinces you to buy twice as much of something that's going to spoil before you can eat it, or junk food you wouldn't eat much of anyway, it's time to think about what the word "sale" is doing to your brain.

153

One very common supermarket strategy is using what's called a loss leader. Here's how it works: a store will sell something essential that nearly everyone buys, like bread or milk, for a price so low that they actually *lose* money on the transaction. Why? They know that customers will be drawn in by the deal, and while they're picking up their bread or milk, they'll likely grab other, higher-priced items, leading to a net gain for the store.

DO YOU WANT FRIES WITH THAT?

How many times have you heard that question—or asked it, if you've worked in a restaurant? Upselling, as it's known, is when someone tries to persuade you to buy more, like a larger iced mocha or a meal combo. While it's frowned upon in some types of business deals, it's very common in restaurants, from fast-food all the way to upscale. Many restaurants train their servers in upselling techniques, or even require them to push customers toward the bigger meal or extra side dish (like super-sizing, or adding fries or soup to an order). For servers, it can be a tricky balance between keeping their managers happy and not being too pushy!

FOOD FOR THOUGHT

As a teenager, you probably see ads for food more often, and in more places, than adults do. There are reasons advertisers pay particular attention to teens: they know you're social creatures, and when you really like a restaurant or brand, you might let your friends know about it, too. They might think younger people are more willing than an older generation to try new things. And they might hope you'll be a lifelong customer if they can win you over now. But it's up to you to decide how much influence you want food marketers to have in your life.

Count how many food ads or messages you see in a day: on TV, online, through your phone, on billboards. How many are for what you'd describe as healthy food?

Make a marketing remix: clip out package labels, magazine ads, or slogans for food, and collage them together with photos or drawings. Does it make you see food advertising in a different way?

Try a simple experiment to test the effect of browser cookies: spend 15 minutes or so looking at web pages for something you wouldn't normally search for—say, how to make pickles. The next time you're online, watch and see how many ads for pickling supplies start showing up!

You might enjoy keeping up with your favorite brands, but be cautious about giving out cell phone numbers or other personal information to companies. You never know how they'll use your information, or whether it will be kept private.

CHAPTER 6

FOOD RULES!

IN THE EARLY 1900S, American writer Upton Sinclair went under-cover in Chicago's meatpacking plants. The information he gathered became the basis of a novel called *The Jungle*, published in 1906. Sinclair had intended to expose the exploitation of factory workers, but what outraged American readers were the accounts of contamination in the packing process. The book was fiction, but many of the conditions it exposed were fact, from dirty factories and workers not washing their hands to moldy and rotting meat, rat droppings, poison, and even whole rats ground up into sausages. Public outcry about the revelations eventually led to the creation of the Food and Drug Administration, which supervises food safety, and a whole system of food regulation and labeling. (In Canada, the role is filled by the Canadian Food Inspection Agency.)

Meatpacking is still considered the most dangerous factory job in the U.S. Workers often cut themselves and sometimes even lose limbs in machinery as they try to keep up with fast line speeds. When Sinclair wrote "The Jungle," meatpacking workers were often poor European immigrants. Today, many workers are immigrants from Latin America and Africa.

Sinclair's book made people aware of the dangers in the food supply, and today, we rely on the government to keep our food safe. But there are debates about how big a role government should play. Some food producers, manufacturers, and restaurants say food regulations are too intrusive, adding extra costs that are then passed on to the consumer. Others say the regulations are not nearly strong enough; these people believe government should do more to keep consumers safe.

KEEPING US SAFE

WE'VE COME A LONG WAY from the days of rat sausages and moldy meat. Today there are all sorts of laws and practices that help keep our food safe, whether it's best-before dates on packages, better technology for food processing, new knowledge about how to safely store and prepare food, or gloves and hairnets for food workers. There are thousands of food inspectors in North America working in factories, farms, and plants every day to keep food safe, and precautions and surveillance are in place to prevent potential terrorist attacks on the food supply. And the advances keep coming—food safety technology gets more and more sophisticated, from microwave processing to extend shelf life to computer modeling of how microbes grow. Because of all these things, over the years there's been a huge drop in the number of people who get sick and die because of food contamination.

MAKING US SICK

DESPITE HOW FAR WE'VE COME, food still needs to be handled with care. Contamination can happen at every stage from the farm to your plate. It can be caused by improper handling, storage, or cooking, and can come from bacteria and viruses, parasites, molds, toxins, and other contaminants. The Centers for Disease Control estimates that in the U.S. alone, there are 48 million cases of illness from food every year, including 128,000 hospitalizations and 3,000 deaths. Most of the millions of people will completely recover after a few unpleasant days. But some groups, like children and older people, are more likely to get seriously sick.

In North America, we can thank our food-safety systems for the fact that there are very few serious, large-scale incidents of contaminated food. When someone does get sick, or contamination is suspected, federal, state and provincial, and local agencies collect information, look for the source, and issue warnings and recalls. You can go on the websites for the USDA and the Canadian Food Inspection Agency to find out about current recalls—where they are, which products are affected, how serious the risk is, and whether they've caused any illnesses or reactions.

DEADLY EFFECTS

Food-borne illnesses can be extremely deadly in developing countries, where regulations aren't always strong as in North America. In the 1970s, a shipment of grain that was meant to be used as seed, not eaten directly, made its way to market in Iraq. The seed was contaminated with a fungus-killing chemical containing mercury, and killed at least 650 people and led to worldwide tightening of food regulations. In 2008, Chinese milk and infant formula contaminated with a chemical called melamine killed 6 children and sickened hundreds of thousands of others. And in India in 2013, 23 students died from eating tainted school meals. Someone had stored the cooking oil in a container that had previously held pesticides.

In 1984, followers of a spiritual leader in a small Oregon city tried to skew the results of a local election—by knocking out most of the population through the food supply! They sprinkled salmonella bacteria over produce in grocery stores and salad bars in restaurants, causing 751 people to fall ill with diarrhea, vomiting, and abdominal cramps. Thankfully no one died, and the harebrained election scheme didn't work, either. But the incident still stands as the largest bioterrorist attack in U.S. history.

SAFETY TIPS

Many food-related illnesses come from improper handling in the kitchen at home. Here are some ways you can reduce your risk:

* Wash your hands well with soap and warm water before and after touching food. Wash counters, cutting boards, and utensils, too.

* Keep raw meat separate from vegetables and cooked foods, and wash any cutting boards, utensils, or plates that came into contact with raw meat. Always make sure meat is properly cooked (a food thermometer can help).

* Wash fruits and vegetables with water—even things like melons and avocados with an inedible skin, because you can transfer bacteria from the outside to the inside while cutting. Experts say it's even a good idea to wash a banana before eating—think how many other hands have touched it before yours!

* Keep hot food hot and cold food cold; temperatures in the middle encourage bacterial growth. Use the two-hour rule: don't keep perishable food at room temperature for more than two hours. If the temperature is over 32 degrees Celsius (90 degrees Fahrenheit), one hour is the limit.

WHAT'S IN THAT PACKAGE?

SOMETIMES IT'S NOT THE FOOD ITSELF but the package it comes in that can make people sick. One chemical that's been getting a lot of attention lately is bisphenol A, or BPA. It's used in many plastics, including water bottles and food containers, as well as to coat the inside of bottle tops, metal cans (if you see a white lining inside a can, it most likely contains BPA), and even paper cups like the ones at coffee shops.

A few years ago, consumers started to worry when research linked BPA to all sorts of health problems, including attention deficit hyperactivity disorder (ADHD) in kids, developmental problems in fetuses, and certain forms of cancer. (Other chemicals in plastics, like phthalates, have been linked to similar issues.) Environmental groups said BPA in packaging could leach into the food or drinks inside them, and argued that the chemical should be banned. One study in Canada showed that 95 percent of the population had some BPA in their blood or urine, with kids having the highest levels. BPA can't be used in baby bottles in Canada, and lots of plastic bottles and cans now advertise that they're BPA free.

163

The Food and Drug Administration and Health Canada believe the amount of BPA we get through food is very low, and people shouldn't be worried about it, but they're continuing to study the chemical. If you're concerned, there are a few things you can do to cut down your exposure to BPA and other chemicals in plastic:

 USE GLASS, STAINLESS STEEL, OR PORCELAIN dishes and utensils whenever you can.

 LOOK ON THE BOTTOM OF PLASTIC CONTAINERS for the little number inside the recycling symbol. Numbers 3 and 7 are likely to contain BPA. Numbers 2, 4, and 5 are safer.

 USE PARCHMENT PAPER OR ALUMINUM FOIL to store food instead of plastic wrap. If you do use plastic wrap, try not to let it touch the food (by putting it over a bowl, for example).

 DON'T MICROWAVE OR FREEZE FOOD IN PLASTIC, or put plastic dishes and containers in the dishwasher. More chemicals seep out of the plastic when it's heated or cooled. Throw out any plastic containers that are cracked or cloudy looking.

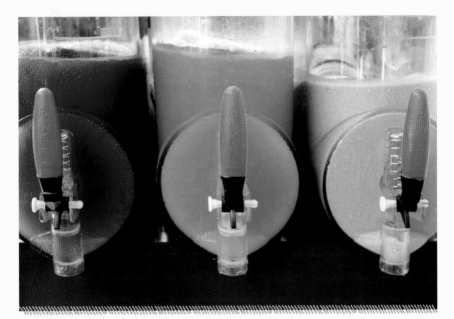

BANNED
SUBSTANCES

WHEN IT COMES TO FOOD, sometimes the danger isn't
from a chemical like BPA, or even from a food-borne
illness. Sometimes the danger lurks in what can happen
down the road, after years of poor food choices. There's a lot of
disagreement about what governments should do about foods that
might cause health problems over the long term. Are our lawmakers
responsible for protecting us from making unhealthy decisions about
what we eat? Those who say "yes" point out that when people get sick
from bad diets, our health-care systems and society bear the costs.
(And those costs are huge: health care costs connected to obesity-
related diseases in the U.S. are estimated at around $117 billion per
year.) They say that junk food is addictive, and should be regulated,
restricted, or taxed, much like tobacco and alcohol are. They also argue
that corporations with huge marketing budgets already have a big

influence over what we eat, so the idea that we make completely independent choices about food is an illusion.

On the "no" side of the debate are people who believe we should be free to make our own decisions about food, even if they're bad ones. They say that choosing what to eat is an essential part of personal freedom, and they don't like the idea of governments influencing or restricting what they eat.

The biggest debates center on a few controversial foods:

✳ **TRANS FATS:** Most nutrition experts consider a safe amount of trans fat to be no trans fat at all, and argue it should be banned. (See chapter 3 for more about trans fats.) Many countries, including the U.S. and Canada, require the amount of trans fat to be included on food labels, and some restrict amounts that can be used in food. Several European countries ban it completely. In the U.S., various cities, counties, and states have banned or restricted trans fat use in restaurants.

✳ **SUGARY DRINKS:** In 2012, New York became the first U.S. city to propose a ban on sugary drinks over 473 milliliters (16 ounces), including soft drinks and convenience store slushees. The mayor and health officials argued that these drinks contributed to weight gain and health problems. However, the ban faced a lot of opposition from beverage companies and consumer groups, who argued it would violate freedom of choice and treat all citizens like children who need their diets monitored. The ban faced several legal challenges, and in 2014 the state's highest court struck it down for good, saying the city's health board had overstepped its authority.

ENERGY DRINKS: Energy drinks are sweetened beverages that contain some type of stimulant, like caffeine, along with herbal extracts and flavorings. Once used mainly by clubbers wanting to dance into the wee hours, or university students pulling all-nighters, they're now popular with young people looking for a jolt of energy, and are promoted as a cool alternative to coffee.

Energy drinks (popular brands include Red Bull and Monster Energy) are controversial because of the amount of caffeine they contain and the fact that they're marketed primarily to young people—their biggest purchasers are people between the ages of 13 and 35. Caffeine is a widely consumed ingredient, found in coffee, tea, some soft drinks, and chocolate. But it's also a strong stimulant that can cause serious side effects. Kids' and teens' bodies can't handle as much caffeine as adults' can, and the American Academy of Pediatrics says young people shouldn't consume energy drinks at all. They've been linked to an increase in emergency-room visits and even a number of deaths of teens and young adults. They can also be especially dangerous in combination with alcohol or other drugs.

Part of the debate centers on whether energy drinks and shots should be classified as health products, foods, or drugs, which are sold and regulated differently. They are most often sold like soft drinks,

Energy shots, a more concentrated form of energy drinks, pack a large amount of caffeine into a very small package. Since you can drink them much faster than a coffee, some doctors warn they can raise your caffeine levels dangerously fast—and drinking more than one will put you over your recommended caffeine limit for the day.

INFOBITES
FOOD-BORNE ILLNESSES

NUMBER OF PEOPLE WHO GET SICK FROM FOOD-BORNE ILLNESSES EVERY YEAR:

U.S.: 1 in 6 Americans

Canada: 1 in 8 Canadians

All industrialized countries: 1 in 3 people

FOOD INSPECTION

NUMBER OF CHICKENS AN INSPECTOR IN AN INDUSTRIAL POULTRY PLANT HAS TO EXAMINE FOR VISUAL SIGNS OF CONTAMINATION, PER SECOND:

In the U.S. **2.3**

In Canada **3.3**

ENERGY DRINKS

SALES OF ENERGY DRINKS IN U.S.

2001
8
million

2012
12.5
billion

TYPICAL SIZE OF ENERGY DRINK

1990s
250 mL
(8.4 oz)

Today
473 mL
(16 oz)

Largest available can, from Monster Energy:
946 mL (32 oz)

NUMBER OF U.S. EMERGENCY ROOM VISITS RELATED TO ENERGY DRINKS:
2005: 1,128   2009: 13,114

which might make people think they pose no more danger than a can of Pepsi. But some health advocates have argued they should be sold in pharmacies like drugs, that people under 18 should be banned from buying them, and that the government should crack down on companies marketing to teens and distributing free samples. The beverage industry, however, says that everyone—including teens—should be free to buy energy drinks and shots if they want to.

ON THE MENU

MAYBE IT'S BECAUSE WE'RE BUSY, or because we don't like to cook every day, but whatever the reason, North Americans today eat way more of their meals in restaurants than ever before. This can be a problem if you're trying to eat well, because you don't always know what goes into restaurant meals, as opposed to when you cook food with fresh ingredients at home. Restaurant dishes tend to have a lot of calories, saturated fat, salt, and sugar—much more than people would think.

That's why health experts have argued that menu labeling is necessary, saying it's important to give teens, kids, and parents the tools to make healthier choices. In the U.S., there are now laws that force restaurant chains to post information about calories and nutrition on their menus. In some Canadian provinces, restaurants

voluntarily put nutrition information on their websites or in brochures (and there are proposed laws that would require this). Does menu labeling actually affect whether diners choose a veggie stir-fry over deep-fried chicken strips? We're still not sure. But some restaurants recognize that being open with their customers about what's in their food can be good for business. Subway, for instance, has successfully branded itself as a company that helps people live healthy lifestyles, and posts detailed nutrition information about their sandwiches and salads in their restaurants and online.

SUE ME!

Should people be able to hold food manufacturers responsible for their poor health? The results of several ongoing lawsuits could provide the answer, and possibly land fast-food companies in deep trouble. In 2013, a New York man sued four fast-food chains— McDonald's, Burger King, KFC, and Wendy's—saying their greasy food contributed to his excess weight, diabetes, and two heart attacks. He claimed the restaurants didn't disclose what was in their food, or advise customers that it wasn't healthy to eat too much of it.

It's a difficult case to make if you believe people make their own choices about what they eat. But if research confirms that sugar and fatty foods are addictive, as some nutritionists suggest, that could open the door to more lawsuits. After tobacco was proven to be addictive, lawsuits cost cigarette companies hundreds of billions of dollars in compensation for deaths, illnesses, and medical expenses caused by smoking. When you consider that the U.S. Department of Health and Human Services attributes more than half a million deaths in the U.S. each year to unhealthy eating, you can imagine the lawsuits piling up!

FOOD FOR THOUGHT

Food regulation is a hot topic, and will probably continue to be in the future. In North America, we've done a good job of ensuring our food supply is safe. Although there are always risks, you can be pretty sure the food you bring home from the grocery store won't contain rat poison or deadly bacteria. But it's harder to know how to deal with things that could put our health in danger at some unknown time in the future. Is the answer government control, or self-control? While lawmakers, public-health experts, and the food industry battle it out, here are some things you can do to stay safe:

Look for the amount of trans fats on labels, and ask restaurants if they cook with trans fats. Find out if your city has any regulations about trans fat usage in restaurants.

Ask to see nutrition information for restaurant dishes, if it's not provided on the menu.

Be cautious with energy drinks: they may look exactly like a can of pop, but they have a much stronger effect on your body. If you do decide to drink them, choose a small size, keep it to one a day, and don't mix them with other substances.

Avoid eating at restaurants or buying from grocery stores that don't seem clean or that have expired products on their shelves. If the areas they let you see are dirty, just imagine the kitchens and backrooms you don't see!

CHAPTER 7

WHAT'S ON YOUR PLATE?

WHAT WILL WE EAT 10 YEARS FROM NOW, or 50, or 100? Food has changed so much in the last century, and even in the last decade. Will we continue on the same path? Will the food of the future look more like the food of the past? Or will it be something we can't imagine yet?

In the 2008 movie *Wall·E*, set several centuries in the future, overconsumption has turned Earth into a barren wasteland covered in garbage. (Yes, this film is intended as fun family entertainment!) People have fled the planet to live on an enormous luxury spaceship, where they spend all day zipping around on floating chairs and growing weak and blob-like thanks to a diet of artificial cupcake–smoothies. It's a vision of food, and life, completely disconnected from the natural world and from what makes us human.

But maybe the future doesn't have to be so bleak. Today, there are signs that people want to feel more connected to their food, whether it's a rise in backyard chicken coops, local farmers' markets, or groups working to improve food security around the world. If you're interested in planting a community garden, learning to cook healthy dishes from different countries, or lobbying your school for decent cafeteria food, there's never been a better time, or more resources and people who can help you get started.

First, let's step back and think about our food situation today.

In 1994, there were only around 1,700 farmers' markets in the entire U.S. Twenty years later, there were over 8,000! There are also 18,000 community gardens in the U.S. and Canada.

BACK TO BASICS

NO CHANGES IN THE HISTORY OF PEOPLE AND FOOD have been more dramatic than what we've seen over the last 70 years or so. We've developed artificial insemination of animals, genetic engineering of crops, ever more effective fertilizers and pesticides, and a whole array of chemical flavorings, additives, and preservatives. Partly because of these innovations, more people today have secure, safe access to food than at any time in human history, not to mention more options and variety in what we eat. But food has gone from something we were closely involved with to something usually grown and produced by strangers, far away.

And yet, we're still animals and we need to eat—and what we eat still usually has to come from a plant or an animal, if you trace it all the way back. Even though many of us live in cities, we depend on the natural world to grow and raise our food, exactly as our ancestors did.

DESERTS AND SWAMPS

EATING FRESH, HEALTHY, LOCAL FOOD SOUNDS GOOD, but it's not so easy if you don't have grocery stores nearby, or if you can't afford the prices at farmers' markets. Unfortunately, this is a reality for many people today, even in countries where food is plentiful.

Many North Americans live in what have been called food deserts: low-income communities without easy access to fresh fruits and vegetables and other healthy foods. In the U.S., about 2.3 million people live more than a 20-minute walk from a supermarket, and don't own a car.

INFOBITES
FOOD INSECURITY

IN 2012 IN THE U.S.:

48.8 million people lived in food-insecure households
11.3 million adults lived in households with very low food security
16.2 million children lived in food-insecure households

NUMBER OF CHILDREN WHO DON'T HAVE CONSISTENT ACCESS TO ADEQUATE FOOD:

U.S.: 1 in 4   Canada: 1 in 5

FOOD DESERTS

NUMBER OF PEOPLE WHO LIVE IN FOOD DESERTS IN THE U.S.:

23.5 million

Of those people, 13.5 million are low-income

For every 1 supermarket in the U.S., there are 5 fast-food restaurants

ORGANIC FOOD

ORGANIC FOOD SALES IN THE U.S.:

1990	2000	2010	2014
$	$ $ $ $ $ $	$ $ $ $ $ $	$ $ $ $ $ $
			$ $ $ $ $ $
			$ $ $ $ $ $
$1 BILLION	**$6 BILLION**	**$27 BILLION**	**$42 BILLION**

Different parts of North America can have extreme differences in food prices. A bag of potatoes that would sell for less than $5 in the rest of the U.S. or Canada costs at least $10 in the North, where a grocery bill of $600 a week to feed a family of three isn't uncommon. In Hawaii, where almost 90 percent of groceries are imported, a gallon of milk can be as expensive as a bottle of wine.

This is often a problem in inner-city neighborhoods, where the only options might be convenience stores. They tend to have higher prices, and their only "fresh" food options might be a few waxy apples and some bruised bananas. Visible minorities, single parents, older people, and those with disabilities are more likely to live in such food deserts.

There are also "food swamps," low-income areas with plenty of fast-food restaurants and convenience stores. The easy availability of unhealthy options at these places has a big influence on the diets of people who live nearby.

Many low-income people are considered "food insecure," which means they can't even count on getting enough food to eat every day, healthy or otherwise. One in four kids in the U.S. is thought to be food insecure. They may depend on a mix of help from neighbors and friends, food stamps, and inexpensive packaged food that's all their parents can afford. In Canada, food insecurity is especially high on Native American reservations and in remote northern communities, where most food has to be brought great distances and can cost at least twice as much as in the rest of the country. For the same reason, food insecurity is higher in the U.S. states of Alaska and Hawaii.

FEEDING THE NORTH

Even though food insecurity is high in northern Canada and Alaska, those regions actually have many natural food resources: Alaska has a multibillion-dollar seafood industry and lots of farmland, for instance, yet the state imports about 95 percent of its food.

In 2012, a state grant in Alaska helped launch a school lunch program aimed at using local foods, like smoked salmon, bison stew, barley cereal, and carrots and snap peas from nearby farms. In addition to being healthier and tastier than prepackaged, heat-and-serve school meals, these options connect Native students to the traditional, non-processed foods eaten by their ancestors, and help reduce their risk of diabetes and heart disease.

Cleaning the daily catch near Seward, Alaska

WHAT'S OLD IS NEW

EVEN THOUGH THE TYPICAL DIET of an American or Canadian is very different now than it was a few generations ago, there are people all over the continent who never abandoned traditional ways of getting food, or who have rediscovered activities like hunting and trapping, fishing, or foraging. In the U.S., reports say nearly 14 million people 16 and older went hunting (for food or sport) sometime in 2012, with most hunting animals like elk, deer, and turkeys. Even more—over 33 million—went fishing.

These activities aren't always cheap: Americans spend around $76 billion a year on hunting and fishing equipment, licenses, and trips! But these statistics are evidence that even though it's a lot easier to drive to the store and buy a shrink-wrapped steak, many people want to be involved in killing and preparing their food themselves.

Food foraging is another ancient practice. Today, foragers gather their own food in the wild—things like mushrooms, fiddleheads, wild leeks, and sea creatures like abalone (an edible type of snail). The new foraging trend was started by people committed to local food, outdoor adventure, and sustainable food sources. But even these simple, traditional methods of harvesting food need to be undertaken in a way that avoids harming the environment. Responsible hunters, fishers, and foragers ensure that they take from nature in quantities that are sustainable, and that they don't remove an important food source for wildlife.

ALL ABOARD THE GROCERY BUS!

One solution to the problem of inner-city food deserts is the mobile market: a truck, bus, or cart delivering fresh, inexpensive produce in neighborhoods that lack access to affordable, healthy food. There's a mobile food market made from a repurposed city bus in Chicago, and other supermarkets-on-the-go are popping up all over North America. These help serve low-income areas where healthy food is hard to come by and beyond the budgets of most residents.

Shopping for produce inside Chicago's Fresh Moves bus

BUGGING OUT

IT'S A FACT: meat takes a lot of land and energy to produce, and the world can't support 7 billion steak-eaters. One solution might be insects—a much more eco-friendly, cheap, and plentiful source of protein than farm animals. True, most North Americans wouldn't be caught dead eating bugs—unless they were taking part in a gross-out challenge! Our aversion to insect consumption isn't shared by all cultures, though; crickets, locusts, ants, and caterpillars are enjoyed in countries all over the world. Indigenous people in Australia eat a type of moth larvae; leafcutter ants are eaten in Colombia and Brazil; mopane worms are popular in southern Africa; and in Cambodia, kids snack on barbecued tarantulas. Some people are trying to make insects more palatable to Westerners: an American company raised funds to produce protein bars made from ground crickets, an Indian restaurant in Vancouver, Canada, offers flatbreads made with cricket flour, and an adventurers' group called the Explorers Club hosts annual dinners with creative insect dishes on the menu.

All of us eat insects, even if we don't think we do. The average chocolate bar contains eight tiny cockroach parts—anything under 60 parts per 100 grams is considered safe. That might sound gross, but it's unavoidable: the cockroaches get into the cocoa beans when they're picked, and trying to get rid of them would require more pesticides, which would be a worse health risk than a few bug parts. And a common red food coloring called cochineal, used in yogurt, drinks, and candies, is made from crushed beetles.

Fried tarantulas are a popular snack in Cambodia.

A Brussels sprout plant is among the many foods grown in this community garden in Brooklyn, N.Y.

HANDS IN THE DIRT

THE MOST DIRECT WAY to get back to basics with food is to grow it yourself. That might sound scary, but it's not! You don't need a huge landscaped garden to get started—merely dirt, water, and a package of seeds. If you live somewhere warm, you can grow some things year-round. If you live somewhere cooler, you might be limited to gardening a few months a year and will have to research what grows well in your area, but there are still many options. You can grow herbs, leafy greens, or sprouts on balconies or sunny windowsills. Backyards or common outdoor spaces for apartment buildings can be used to grow a variety of vegetables, from carrots to kale.

One great thing about growing your own food is that you control what goes into it. It's surprisingly easy to grow a veggie garden with no pesticides or chemicals. You can make bug-fighting sprays with ingredients you probably have in your cupboard, like soap, garlic, and chili pepper. Before you know it, you'll be eating organic, but without the fancy-food prices!

More and more schools across North America are starting gardens, and there are networks that provide resources and assistance for students and teachers. Community gardens, which provide people in a neighborhood with small plots of land to grow vegetables, are also becoming more popular. You can go online to find out if there's a community garden in your area, and if not, you could even approach your city or town about starting one.

Most of us in North America would have trouble growing *all* of our own produce, especially in the winter. But even growing one or two things can make you feel more connected to what you eat, and more accomplished: the first time you plant a seed and see a green shoot pop up a few days later, it can seem like a tiny miracle. You're also more likely to enjoy trying new kinds of vegetables if you grow them yourself.

Want to get your hands really dirty? Today there are opportunities all over the world for young people to volunteer on organic farms, usually working four to six hours a day for a few weeks in exchange for free room and board. Various websites and organizations help pair volunteers with farms that need help with tasks like sowing seeds, picking fruit, or feeding animals. Many people find this a great way to see new places, meet people, support sustainable farming, and learn the ins and outs of growing food.

GANGSTA GARDENING

Ron Finley grew up in South Central Los Angeles, a place he describes as a "food prison," where lack of access to healthy foods was making his community sick. As an adult, tired of driving 45 minutes to the nearest grocery store that sold fresh, organic produce, Finley started his own garden on the curb strip in front of his house, growing a colorful and fragrant mix of tomatoes, peppers, eggplant, pumpkin, lavender, jasmine, and sunflowers. His garden attracted attention from kids and adults in the neighborhood, who were soon helping out and sharing the garden's bounty. When the city told him he had to pay $400 for a permit or remove the garden, Finley collected signatures on an online petition, and finally got the city to relax its laws. Since then, he's helped plant dozens of public gardens, revolutionizing how many residents in the low-income South Central area approach their food.

Ron Finley at one of his curbside gardens

FOOD AT HOME

DO YOU HELP OUT with the cooking and shopping in your house? Many North American teens do, and in countries around the world, kids are expected to be in the kitchen or the fields from a young age. Lots of teens find cooking to be a fun and creative way to learn about food, try interesting new dishes, and gain some skills they'll use the rest of their lives. (It's also a great way to shake up your family's routine, if you're bored of the same old meals your parents always cook.) How to start? You could watch your parents or older siblings in the kitchen, and offer to help with preparing or chopping vegetables. Watch TV cooking shows and YouTube videos, get a beginners' cookbook out of the library, or search online for recipes with photo instructions. Like anything, cooking is a skill that takes practice, and everyone is going to burn their garlic or oversalt their soup once in a while, but it's surprisingly easy to learn to make a few easy and yummy dinners, like pasta with basil pesto and tomatoes, or fish tacos. (But don't get *too* good, or your family might expect you to become their full-time chef!)

Don't be surprised, though, if you find that sitting down to eat your culinary creation is a challenge. In 1900, Americans ate only about 2 percent of their meals away from home.

TODAY | **1900**

50% | **2%**

Today, we eat half our meals out. On average, families only eat together about three times a week, and usually spend just 20 minutes at the table. In the U.S. and Canada we also eat a lot of our food on the go: North America is the birthplace of the car cupholder, after all (and the fast-food meals designed especially to fit in the cupholder!). Many adults and kids eat in cars more often than they eat at home, a habit that encourages people to eat more fast food and sugary drinks.

Families these days can have busy lives, and some eating on the run can't be helped. But all sorts of benefits have been shown when families sit down for dinner together regularly: kids and teens do better in school, have better relationships with other people, and are generally in better health. Taking the time to enjoy food and talk with our families can be a good way to connect after a hectic day.

THRIFTY EATING

People sometimes assume that fast food is cheaper than cooking and eating at home, but that's not always true. A fast-food meal for four people at McDonald's, for instance, costs over $20. But you can make dinner for four in your kitchen using basic grocery-store ingredients for much less: a roasted chicken with potatoes and a salad costs under $15 to prepare, while a meal of rice and beans with sautéed veggies, or spaghetti with tomato sauce and a salad, can be made for well under $10.

FOOD AT SCHOOL

SCHOOL IS WHERE YOU SPEND A BIG PART of your life as a teen, so it's no surprise that you eat about a third of all your daily calories there. Unfortunately, many schools are not usually great places to find fresh and healthy food, or food for vegetarians or those on a special diet. Traditional cafeteria lunches are usually high in sodium and fat, and lacking in fresh vegetables, whole grains, and healthy protein. DoSomething.org ran a campaign asking students to send in photos of their school lunches, and posted the results—featuring plenty of deep-fried food, scary-looking mystery meat, and wilted shreds of iceberg lettuce—on their website. They also provide an online kit with information for students who want to improve their school cafeteria's options.

In the hallways, school vending machines tend to be stocked with sweet drinks, candy, chocolate, and salty chips. Soft drinks in schools

VEGGIE OPTIONS

Going vegetarian might have benefits for your health and society, but it can be hard on your social life. School cafeterias and restaurants may not offer many options, and even going to a friend's house for dinner can get complicated. It's a challenge to be the only person who doesn't eat meat at a barbecue or pizza party, or to quiz bewildered cafeteria workers and restaurant servers about whether there's chicken stock in the vegetable soup, lard in the bean burritos, or marshmallows (made with gelatin) in the Rice Krispies squares. Some vegetarian teens gain strength from banding together with others at school, or online, and asking for clearly labeled veggie options in the cafeteria or in local restaurants. There are also online resources that tell you which items at chain restaurants are veggie-friendly, and many international-food restaurants—Indian, Middle Eastern, Italian, Thai—have good options.

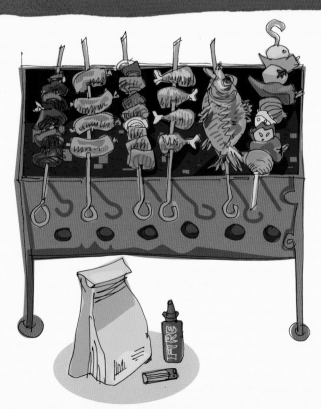

might be a thing of the past, but schools still have contracts with big soft drink companies, like Coca-Cola or Pepsi, which have juice, water, and snack-food subsidiaries. These companies pay schools up to $15,000 in much-needed funds a year for the privilege of supplying their students with the non-carbonated bottled drinks and processed snack foods that fill vending machines. You can find a few healthier options in some vending machines, like bottled water and milk—and there's always the water fountain (where you can refill your own bottle, and save your pocket money for something else).

There have been efforts to improve food in schools over the past years, with mixed results—some schools say their students complain when they serve better-balanced cafeteria meals, or replace chips and candy with fresh fruit. But some schools have had great success. In 2013, one elementary school cafeteria in New York City became the first in the country to go completely vegetarian. The school serves freshly made lunches like black bean quesadillas, falafels, roasted tofu, and brown rice, and about 90 percent of the students eat in the cafeteria rather than bringing lunches from home. Since the change, school administrators have reported that kids have longer attention spans and are getting better grades.

HAIL TO THE CHEFS

One of the most interesting efforts to improve school lunches is the Cooking up Change challenge, in which teams of student chefs in 10 cities in the U.S. compete to create delicious, nutritious, creative school lunch menus for around a dollar per meal. Every year the winning teams travel to Washington, D.C., to meet with lawmakers and discuss the changes needed to get more healthy food into schools.

People concerned about unsafe genetic modification of foods take to the streets in Los Angeles in 2014.

FOOD ALL AROUND YOU

YOU CAN ALSO HAVE AN EFFECT on the food beyond your home and school. Local grocery stores and independent neighborhood restaurants are likely to listen if you tell them you'd like to see different options, or if you politely ask questions, like where their fish comes from, whether they have any local produce, or what they do with their food waste. These companies want to keep customers happy, and sometimes it takes only a small number of people to request a product, or express a concern, in order to make a change.

Even big companies and organizations can listen if enough of us make noise—or sometimes even if one person makes a really big noise.

People who are still too young to vote have made some stunning achievements in the food industry. In 2014, a 17-year-old girl in Mississippi named Sarah Kavanagh convinced Coca-Cola and PepsiCo to remove brominated vegetable oil (BVO)—which can cause nerve disorders, and has been banned in many countries—from their energy drinks. She started a petition on the website Change.org and gathered over 200,000 signatures before the companies decided to replace the BVO with another ingredient. A Canadian high-school student named Rachel Parent has become one of the strongest voices supporting labeling of genetically modified foods, and has even debated adult news reporters—much less informed about the issues than she was—on national TV. In Virginia, Nina Gonzales talked to everyone from lunch-line workers to the county's nutrition director to get more vegan options into her school cafeteria, and appeared before the U.S. Senate to speak about healthy school meals. And Beebe Sanders in California helps run a program that improves her community's access to fresh produce.

Activist Rachel Parent has become a powerful voice in the movement to label genetically modified foods.

These are only a few of the young people making their voices heard about the kind of food they want to eat and the kind of world they want to live in. Imagine what could be achieved if more voices join in.

STEP UP!

The old saying that "the perfect is the enemy of the good" rings especially true where food is concerned. Basically, it means that focusing too much on trying to reach an ideal can make it impossible for you to do anything positive at all. In terms of food, sure, it would be great if we could all eat organic, locally harvested, free-range, lovingly prepared gourmet food 100 percent of the time. But just because most of us will never achieve that, it doesn't mean that whatever small steps you can take aren't worthwhile. Cooking a meal at home once a week, even if you don't have pricey organic ingredients, is better than never. Buying one locally grown food, if you can, is better than none. And signing a petition, or even reading up on an issue, is better than doing nothing. It's all about finding little ways to make a difference, one step at a time.

FOOD FOR THOUGHT

It's a great time to be interested in eating well. Sure, the majority of the food in our supermarkets and restaurants still comes from food production methods that may not be sustainable over the long term, for the environment or our health. Yet there are more alternatives now in North America than ever before: farmers' markets and food delivery trucks offering fresh, local produce; healthier options at fast-food restaurants that used to have none; organic, vegetarian, and allergy-sensitive products on supermarket shelves.

There are many organizations working to improve food in various ways, and topics like food deserts, sustainability, and healthy school lunches—issues few people had even thought about not long ago—are now being discussed and debated regularly by politicians. Things are changing, in ways big and small. You can be part of that change, too.

What Can You Do Right Now?

Visit a farmer's market or try to get your teacher to organize a class trip to a local farm.

Tell your school cafeteria, local restaurants, fast-food chains, and grocery stores that you want to see more healthy, local, organic, or vegetarian options.

Follow the issues you feel strongly about, whether it's food insecurity in your state or province, or animal welfare in the farm industry. Start or sign petitions, or get involved in other ways.

FURTHER READING

Elton, Sarah. *Starting From Scratch: What You Should Know About Food and Cooking*. Toronto: Owlkids, 2014.

Gold, Rozanne. *Eat Fresh Food: Awesome Recipes for Teen Chefs*. New York: Bloomsbury, 2009.

Locricchio, Matthew. *Teen Cuisine*. Tarrytown, NY: Marshall Cavendish, 2014.

Melina, Vesanto, and Brenda Davis. *The New Becoming Vegetarian: The Essential Guide to a Healthy Vegetarian Diet*. Summertown, TN: Healthy Living Publications, 2003.

Nestle, Marion. *What to Eat*. New York: North Point Press, 2007.

Pleasant, Barbara. *Starter Vegetable Gardens: 24 No-Fail Plans for Small Organic Gardens*. North Adams, MA: Storey, 2010.

Richard, Sandi. *Anyone Can Cook Dinner*. St. Catharines, ON: Cooking for the Rushed Inc., 2012.

Singer, Peter, and Jim Mason. *The Ethics of What We Eat: Why Our Food Choices Matter*. Emmaus, Penn.: Rodale, 2007.

Trail, Gayla. *You Grow Girl: The Groundbreaking Guide to Gardening*. New York: Fireside, 2005.

IMAGE CREDITS

SELECTED SOURCES

Chapter 1

Crosby, Alfred W. "Columbian Exchange: Plants, Animals, and Disease Between the Old and New World." *The Encyclopedia of Earth*, Feb. 19, 2009, updated March 29, 2013, eoearth. org/view/article/151313

Dunn, Robb. "Human Ancestors Were Nearly All Vegetarian." *Scientific American* blogs, Jul. 23, 2012, blogs.scientificamerican.com/guest-blog/2012/07/23/human-ancestors-were-nearly-all-vegetarians/

Food and Agriculture Organization of the United Nations. "The State of Food Insecurity in the World 2014." fao.org/publications/sofi/en/

Gara, Tom. "Online Shopping Is Big. It's Also Tiny." *Corporate Intelligence* (blog), *The Wall Street Journal* online, Feb. 26, 2014, blogs.wsj.com/corporate-intelligence/2014/02/26/online-shopping-is-big-its-also-tiny/

Garber, Megan. "The 20 Most Significant Inventions in the History of Food and Drink." *The Atlantic* online, Sep. 14, 2012, theatlantic.com/technology/archive/2012/09/the-20-most-significant-inventions-in-the-history-of-food-and-drink/262410/

Government of Canada. "Food in Canada." Statistics Canada website. statcan.gc.ca/pub/16-201-x/2009000/part-partie1-eng.htm

Groceteria.com. "A Quick History of the Supermarket." groceteria.com/about/a-quick-history-of-the-supermarket/

"Historical Timeline—Farmers and the Land." *Growing a Nation: The Story of American Agriculture* (website). www.agclassroom.org/gan/timeline/farmers_land.htm

Kiple, Kenneth F. *A Movable Feast: Ten Millennia of Food Globalization*. Cambridge: Cambridge University Press, 2007.

Lacey, Richard W. *Hard to Swallow: A Brief History of Food*. Cambridge: Cambridge University Press, 2008.

Olver, Lynne. "The Food Timeline." Last updated Sep. 21, 2014. foodtimeline.org

Rasmussen, Wayne D. "Origins of Agriculture." In *Encyclopædia Britannica Online*, last modified Mar. 17, 2014, britannica.com/EBchecked/topic/9647/agriculture

Steel, Carolyn. "How Food Shapes Our Cities" (video). TED website, July 2009, ted.com/talks/carolyn_steel_how_food_shapes_our_cities.html

Thompson, Derek. "How America Spends Money: 100 Years in the Life of the Family Budget." *The Atlantic* online, Apr. 5, 2012, theatlantic.com/business/archive/2012/04/how-america-spends-money-100-years-in-the-life-of-the-family-budget/255475/

World Food Programme. "Hunger statistics." wfp.org/hunger/stats

Chapter 2

Chea, Terence. "Michael Pollan, Farmers, & OCA Speak Out on 'Big Organic.'" Organic Consumers Association website, May 30, 2006, organicconsumers.org/articles/article_586.cfm

CNN Staff. "FDA Hopes to Curb Antibiotic Use on Farms." *CNN Health*, Dec. 12, 2013, cnn.com/2013/12/11/health/fda-antibiotics-farms/

Environmental Working Group. "EWG's 2014 Shopper's Guide to Pesticides in Produce." ewg.org/foodnews/summary.php

Eshel, Gidon, Alon Shepon et al. "Land, Irrigation Water, Greenhouse Gas, and Reactive Nitrogen Burdens of Meat, Eggs, and Dairy Production in the United States." *Proceedings of the National Academy of Sciences* 111, no. 33: 11996–12001. doi: 10.1073/pnas.1402183111.

Foer, Jonathan Safran. *Eating Animals*. New York: Little, Brown and Company, 2009.

Gerber, P.J., H. Steinfeld, et al. *Tackling Climate Change Through Livestock: A Global Assessment of Emissions and Mitigation Opportunities* (report). Rome: Food and Agriculture Organization of the United Nations, 2013, fao.org/docrep/018/i3437e/i3437e.pdf

Gibson, Stacey. "The Lives of Animals." *U of T Magazine*, Autumn 2010, magazine.utoronto.ca/feature/ethics-of-raising-livetock-industrial-agriculture-animal-rights-u-of-t/

Government of Canada. "Pesticides and Food." Health Canada website, last updated Jul. 2, 2013, hc-sc.gc.ca/cps-spc/pubs/pest/_fact-fiche/pesticide-food-alim/index-eng.php

Gurian-Sherman, Doug. *CAFOs Uncovered: The Untold Costs of Confined Animal Feeding Operations.* Union of Concerned Scientists website, Apr. 2008, ucsusa.org/assets/documents/food_and_agriculture/cafos-uncovered-executive-summary.pdf

Hoffmann, Irene. "Climate Change and the Characterization, Breeding and Conservation of Animal Genetic Resources." *Animal Genetics* 41 (May 2010), Suppl. 1: 32-46. doi: 10.1111/j.1365-2052.2010.02043.x.

The Humane Society of the United States. "Anti-Whistleblower Bills Hide Factory-Farming Abuses from the Public." Mar. 25, 2014, humanesociety.org/issues/campaigns/factory_farming/fact-sheets/ag_gag.html#id=album-185&num=content-3312

James, Deborah. "Food Security, Farming, and the WTO and CAFTA." Global Exchange website, accessed Feb. 18, 2014, globalexchange.org/resources/wto/agriculture

Kiernan, Bill. "Grass Fed Versus Corn Fed: You Are What Your Food Eats." Global AgInvesting website, Jul. 16, 2012, globalaginvesting.com/news/blogdetail?contentid=1479

Lang, Tim. "Food Industrialization and Food Power: Implications for Food Governance (report)." International Institute for Environment and Development, Natural Resources Group and Sustainable Agriculture and Rural Livelihoods Programme, Gatekeeper Series No. 114, June 2004, dlc.dlib.indiana.edu/dlc/bitstream/handle/10535/6192/food%20industrialisation.pdf?sequence=1

Levasseur, Joanne, and Vera-Lynn Kubinec. "Pesticide residue found on nearly half of organic produce." *CBC News* online, Jan. 8, 2014, cbc.ca/news/canada/manitoba/pesticide-residue-found-on-nearly-half-of-organic-produce-1.2487712

McKenna, Maryn. "Antibiotic-Resistant Bacteria Surround Big Swine Farms—In China as Well as the U.S." *Superbug* (blog), *Wired* online, Feb. 12, 2013, wired.com/wiredscience/2013/02/china-resistance-hogs/

McKie, Robin. "How the Myth of Food Miles Hurts the Planet." *The Observer, The Guardian* online, Mar. 23, 2008, theguardian.com/environment/2008/mar/23/food.ethicalliving

Philpott, Tom. "How food processing got into the hands of a few giant companies." *Grist*, Apr. 27, 2007, grist.org/article/giants/

Pollan, Michael. "We Are What We Eat." Center for Ecoliteracy website, accessed Feb. 15, 2014, ecoliteracy.org/essays/we-are-what-we-eat

Rosner, Hillary. "Palm Oil and Scout Cookies: The Battle Drags On." *Green* (blog), *The New York Times* online, Feb. 13, 2012, green.blogs.nytimes.com/2012/02/13/palm-oil-and-scout-cookies-the-battle-drags-on/?_php=true&_type=blogs&_php=true&_type=blogs&_r=1

Siebert, Charles. "Food Ark." *National Geographic* online, July 2011, ngm.nationalgeographic.com/2011/07/food-ark/siebert-text/1

Simon, David Robinson. *Meatonomics.* San Francisco: Conari Press, 2013.

Starmer, Elanor. "Corporate Power in Livestock Production." The Agribusiness Accountability Initiative, *Leveling the Field*—Issue Brief 1 (newsletter), ase.tufts.edu/gdae/Pubs/rp/AAI_Issue_Brief_1_3.pdf

Stuckler, David, and Marion Nestle. "Big Food, Food Systems, and Global Health." *PLoS Medicine* 9(6): e1001242 (Jun. 19, 2012). doi:10.1371/journal.pmed.1001242.

Tidwell, James H., and Geoff L. Allan. "Fish as Food: Aquaculture's Contribution." *EMBO Rep.* 2, no. 11 (Nov. 15, 2001): 958–963. doi: 10.1093/embo-reports/kve236.

Vancouver Aquarium. "Sustainable Seafood." Ocean Wise, oceanwise.ca/about/sustainable-seafood

Chapter 3

"The Big Fat Truth About Fat." *O Magazine* online, Mar. 2004, oprah.com/omagazine/
The-Big-Fat-Truth-About-Fat/

Centers for Disease Control and Prevention. "Childhood Obesity Facts." CDC website, Aug. 13,
2014, cdc.gov/healthyyouth/obesity/facts.htm

Chen, Linda. "The Old And Mysterious Practice Of Eating Dirt, Revealed." *The Salt*
(blog), NPR online, Apr. 2, 2014, npr.org/blogs/thesalt/2014/04/02/297881388/
the-old-and-mysterious-practice-of-eating-dirt-revealed

Cohen, Rich. "Sugar." *National Geographic* online, Aug. 2013, ngm.nationalgeographic.
com/2013/08/sugar/cohen-text

European Food Information Council. "Understanding Scientific Studies." EUFIC website, Jan.
2008, eufic.org/article/en/page/RARCHIVE/expid/Understanding-scientific-studies/

Grant, Kelly. "WHO to Propose Lower Recommended Daily Limit for Sugar Intake."
The Globe and Mail online, Mar. 4, 2014, theglobeandmail.com/news/national/
who-to-work-on-lowering-recommended-daily-limit-for-sugar-intake/article17311412/

Groopman, Jerome. "The Peanut Puzzle." *The New Yorker*, Feb. 7, 2011, 26–30.

Harvard School of Public Health. "Healthy Eating Plate & Healthy Eating Pyramid." The Nutrition
source, accessed Mar. 4, 2014, hsph.harvard.edu/nutritionsource/healthy-eating-plate/

Johnson, Patrick. "Obesity: Epidemic or Myth?" *Skeptical Inquirer* 29.5 (Sept–Oct. 2005), csicop.
org/si/show/obesity_epidemic_or_myth/

Knapton, Sarah. "Saturated Fat Is Not Bad for Health, Says Heart Expert." *The Telegraph* online,
Mar. 6, 2014, telegraph.co.uk/health/healthnews/10679227/Saturated-fat-is-not-bad-for-
health-says-heart-expert.html

Langlois, Kellie, and Didier Garriguet. "Sugar Consumption Among Canadians of All Ages."
Statistics Canada Health Reports 22, no. 3 (Feb. 18, 2014), statcan.gc.ca/pub/82-
003-x/2011003/article/11540-eng.htm

Levinovitz, Alan. "Hold the MSG." *Slate*, Jul. 9, 2013, slate.com/articles/health_and_science/
medical_examiner/2013/07/msg_and_gluten_intolerance_is_the_nocebo_effect_to_
blame.html

Mosby, Ian. *Food Will Win the War: The Politics, Culture, and Science of Food on Canada's Home
Front*. Vancouver: UBC Press, 2014.

Nagler, Rebekah H. "Adverse Outcomes Associated With Media Exposure to Contradictory
Nutrition Messages." *Journal of Health Communication* 19, no. 1 (2014): 24–40. doi:
10.1080/10810730.2013.798384.

Nestle, Marion. *Food Politics: How the Food Industry Influences Nutrition and Health* (revised
edition). Berkeley: University of California Press, 2013. First published 2002.

PBS Frontline. *Diet Wars*. PBS website, Apr. 8, 2004, pbs.org/wgbh/pages/frontline/shows/diet/

Schwartz, Daniel. "The Politics of Food Guides." CBC News online, Jul. 30, 2012, cbc.ca/news/
health/the-politics-of-food-guides-1.1268575

Szabo, Liz. "Diabetes Rates Skyrocket in Kids and Teens." *USA Today* online, May 3, 2014,
usatoday.com/story/news/nation/2014/05/03/diabetes-rises-in-kids/8604213/

Weintraub, Karen. "Should We Eat Meat?" *The Boston Globe* online, Sep. 9, 2013, bostonglobe.
com/lifestyle/health-wellness/2013/09/08/evidence-shows-that-cutting-down-our-meat-
consumption-would-good-for-why-don/YIFTosUr4Gesg2lLDoSwxK/story.html

Chapter 4

Chen, Adrian. "We Drank Soylent, The Weird Food of the Future." *Gawker*, May 29, 2013, gawker.
com/we-drank-soylent-the-weird-food-of-the-future-510293401

Coghlan, Andy. "What's the Beef? Cultured Meat Remains a Distant Dream." *New Scientist*
online, Aug. 6, 2013, newscientist.com/article/dn23996-whats-the-beef-cultured-meat-
remains-a-distant-dream.html?full=true#.UngID-Be-aA

Contois, Emily. "Curating the History of American Convenience Cuisine." Emily Contois (blog),
Oct. 4, 2012, emilycontois.com/2012/10/04/curating-the-history-of-american-convenience-cuisine/

Delano, Maggie. "Roundup Ready Crops: Cash Crop or Third World Savior?" Massachusetts
Institute of Technology website, 2009, web.mit.edu/demoscience/Monsanto/impact.html

Landau, Elizabeth. "Subway to Remove 'Dough Conditioner' Chemical from Bread." *CNN Health*,
Feb. 17, 2014, cnn.com/2014/02/06/health/subway-bread-chemical/index.html?c&page=2

McCann, Donna, Angelina Barrett, et al. "Food Additives and Hyperactive Behaviour in 3-Year-Old and 8/9-Year-Old Children in the Community: A Randomised, Double-Blinded,
Placebo-Controlled Trial." *The Lancet* 370, no. 9598 (Nov. 3, 2007): 1560–67. doi:10.1016/
S0140-6736(07)61306-3.

Moss, Michael. *Salt, Sugar, Fat: How the Food Giants Hooked Us.* Toronto: McClelland & Stewart,
2013.

Pollan, Michael. "Some of My Best Friends Are Germs." *The New York Times Magazine*, May 15,
2013, nytimes.com/2013/05/19/magazine/say-hello-to-the-100-trillion-bacteria-that-make-up-your-microbiome.html?hp&_r=0

Popovich, Nadja. "Before Soylent: A Brief History of Food Replacements." *The Guardian* online,
Feb. 5, 2014, theguardian.com/lifeandstyle/2014/feb/05/before-soylent-brief-history-food-replacements

Snopes.com. "Aspartame." Feb. 2, 2010, snopes.com/medical/toxins/aspartame.asp

——. "The Dangers of Splenda." Jan. 20, 2014, snopes.com/medical/toxins/splenda.asp

Weeks, Carly. "Is Artificial Food Colouring Really Unsafe? The Jury Is Still Out." *The Globe
and Mail* online, Sep. 17, 2013, theglobeandmail.com/life/health-and-fitness/health/
is-artificial-food-colouring-really-unsafe-the-jury-is-still-out/article14351106/

Chapter 5

Barnes, Robert. "Court to Determine What Constitutes Pomegranate Juice." *The Washington
Post* online, Apr. 21, 2014, washingtonpost.com/politics/court-to-determine-what-constitutes-pomegranate-juice/2014/04/21/e4abc87a-c996-11e3-93eb-6c0037dde2ad_story.
html?utm_source=nextdraft&utm_medium=email

Beacham, Tom. "Globalization and the 'Fast Food' Industry." Centre for Research on Globaliza-tion, Jan. 4, 2014, globalresearch.ca/globalization-and-the-fast-food-industry/5363703

Berkeley Media Studies Group. "The New Age of Food Marketing: How Companies are Targeting
and Luring Our Kids—and What Advocates Can Do About It." Oct. 1, 2011, bmsg.org/
resources/publications/the-new-age-of-food-marketing

Burns, Grainne. "Yogurt: The Most Versatile Grocery Aisle Product." *Marketing Magazine*, Mar. 7,
2014, marketingmag.ca/news/marketer-news/yogurt-the-most-versatile-grocery-aisle-product-103040

Canadian Food Advertising Agency. "Food Labelling and Advertising." inspection.gc.ca/food/
labelling/eng/1299879892810/1299879939872

Center for Science in the Public Interest. "7UP Drops 'All-Natural' Claim." Jan. 12, 2007, cspinet.
org/new/200701121.html

——. "Food Labeling." Accessed Mar. 16, 2014, cspinet.org/foodlabeling/

Klein, Ezra. "Michael Pollan Thinks Wall Street Has Way Too Much Influence Over What We Eat."
Vox, Apr. 23, 2014, vox.com/2014/4/23/5627992/big-food-michael-pollan-thinks-wall-street-has-way-too-much-influence?utm_source=nextdraft&utm_medium=email

Wansink, B. & K. Van Ittersum (2012). "Fast Food Restaurant Lighting and Music Can Reduce
Calorie Intake and Increase Satisfaction." *Psychological Reports: Human Resources &
Marketing* 111, no. 1: 1–5.

Yale Rudd Center for Food Policy and Obesity. *Fast Food F.A.C.T.S. 2013: Measuring Progress in
Nutrition and Marketing to Children and Teens*, fastfoodmarketing.org/media/FastFood-FACTS_Report_Summary.pdf

Chapter 6

BBC News Asia. "School Meal Kills at Least 22 Children in India's Bihar State." Jul. 17, 2013, bbc.co.uk/news/world-asia-23339789

Bottemiller Evich, Helena. "The Plot to Make Big Food Pay." *Politico*, Feb. 12, 2014, politico.com/story/2014/02/food-industry-obesity-health-care-costs-103390.html

Cohen, Adam. "100 Years Later, the Food Industry Is Still 'The Jungle.'" *The New York Times* online, Jan. 2, 2007, nytimes.com/2007/01/02/opinion/02tue4.html?ref=uptonsinclair

Food and Drug Administration. "Bisphenol A (BPA): Use in Food Contact Application." Accessed Mar. 20, 2014, fda.gov/NewsEvents/PublicHealthFocus/ucm064437.htm

Government of Canada. "Bisphenol A." Health Canada website, accessed Mar. 20, 2014, hc-sc.gc.ca/fn-an/securit/packag-emball/bpa/index-eng.php

Grynbaum, Michael. "New York's Ban on Big Sodas Is Rejected by Final Court." *The New York Times* online, Jun. 26, 2014, nytimes.com/2014/06/27/nyregion/city-loses-final-appeal-on-limiting-sales-of-large-sodas.html

Weeks, Carly. "Beverage Branding Gives Energy Drinks Undeserved Stamp of Approval, Critic Says." *The Globe and Mail* online, Mar. 20, 2013, theglobeandmail.com/life/health-and-fitness/health/beverage-branding-gives-energy-drinks-undeserved-stamp-of-approval-critic-says/article10032783/

Zuraw, Lydia. "Reactions Vary to USDA's Poultry Inspection Rule." *Food Safety News*, Aug. 1, 2014, foodsafetynews.com/2014/08/groups-react-to-final-poultry-inspection-rule/#.VCnKOChbkTM

Chapter 7

DeMarban, Alex. "Local Alaska Foods Make Way Into School Lunch Menus." *Alaska Dispatch News*, Nov. 8, 2012, alaskadispatch.com/article/local-alaska-foods-make-way-school-lunch-menus

DoSomething.org. "Fed Up." fedup.dosomething.org/fedup

Health Canada. *Measuring the Food Environment in Canada.* 2013, hc-sc.gc.ca/fn-an/nutrition/pol/index-eng.php

Karstens-Smith, Gemma. "Toronto Food Truck Brings Nutritious Produce to Needy Communities." *Toronto Star*, Dec. 1, 2013, thestar.com/news/gta/2013/12/01/toronto_food_truck_brings_nutritious_produce_to_needy_communities.html

Klein, Debra A. "The Foraging Wars: Extreme Eating Hits California." *The Daily Beast*, Jan. 31, 2014, thedailybeast.com/articles/2014/01/31/the-foraging-wars-extreme-eating-hits-california.html

Rabeler, Katrina. "'Renegade Gardener' Plots World Domination Through Home-Grown Veggies." *Yes!* online, Jul. 30, 2013, yesmagazine.org/people-power/gardening-is-gangsta-an-interview-with-urban-gardener-ron-finley

Salisbury, Peter. "Behind the Brand: McDonald's." *The Ecologist*, Jun. 16, 2011, theecologist.org/green_green_living/behind_the_label/941743/behind_the_brand_mcdonalds.html

Sifferlin, Alexandra. "Can 'Pop-Up' Grocery Stores Solve the Problem of Food Deserts?" *Time* online, Jul. 24, 2012, healthland.time.com/2012/07/24/can-pop-up-grocery-stores-solve-the-problem-of-food-deserts/

Takepart.com. *A Place at the Table: One Nation. Underfed.* takepart.com/place-at-the-table

Trapasso, Claire. "Queens School That Went Vegetarian Shows Student Gains, Draws Plaudit." *New York Daily News* online, Oct. 15, 2013, nydailynews.com/new-york/queens/vegging-better-school-article-1.1486681#ixzz2va8nXoip

United States Department of Agriculture. "Food Access Research Atlas." ers.usda.gov/Data/FoodDesert/#.VCnPJihbkTM

INDEX

ACKNOWLEDGMENTS

Thanks to:

Annick Press, especially Antonia Banyard, who has supported and guided the book in many ways from the very beginning, and provided diligent and creative image research and art direction;

Pam Robertson, for bringing much-needed order, sense, and balance to the manuscript; Linda Pruessen, for expert lightening and tightening; and Tanya Trafford, for cheerful and eagle-eyed proofing;

Natalie Olsen, for her excellent design, and Ira Olenina, for his witty illustrations delivered generously and professionally;

Barbara Emmanuel, for taking time to read the manuscript; and

Shaker Paleja, for his constructive comments on the book and his support through the process of writing it.

ABOUT THE AUTHOR

Paula Ayer grew up in a family of sausage-making Europeans in the middle of Canadian cattle country, and rebelled at age 15 by forsaking animal products. Her husband was raised by Hindu vegetarians, and rebelled in his teens by eating meat. Family gatherings are always complicated, but the dinner table is never empty.

Paula has worked on many books—as an editor, translator, researcher, art director, and even amateur cover model—but this is her first attempt at writing one. She has written other things, including magazine articles, music reviews, advertising copy, and exhaustive blog posts about TV shows. She lives in Vancouver, British Columbia, with her husband and daughter, surrounded by more organic kale than you would ever want to eat.